FROM GRIEF TO GRACE

A THERAPIST'S JOURNEY OF HEALING AFTER LOSS

Anita Salek Aasen LCSW

For Lou,

You are always in my heart.

ACKNOWLEDGMENT

Reflecting on my journey, I feel immense gratitude for those who have supported me during this ongoing process of growth and transformation. It's been a path of constant evolution, shaping who I am today in ways I never anticipated.

First, I want to thank Linda. Her office was my refuge in my darkest times, where I found solace in pouring out my emotions. Her patience and understanding provided the comfort I desperately needed during a period of profound sadness.

I must also acknowledge Pauline, who walked beside me at a pivotal moment just a day before I lost Lou. Her presence was a source of strength as I steered through the initial shock and sorrow.

My classmates from the class of 1975—Anne, Debbie, Christine, Marinella, Dorothy, and Isabel—also deserve recognition. Affectionately known as my "eagles," their camaraderie and encouragement uplifted me during this journey.

I am deeply thankful for all the clients I've had the privilege to work with. Each of you has brought something unique to this experience, and I'm honored to have walked with you through your grief. Your courage has inspired me in ways I never expected, even motivating me to consider writing a book about this journey.

A special thanks goes to my husband, Victor, and my children, Amanda, Krista, and Sara. Their unwavering support has been the cornerstone of my endeavors, propelling me forward as I pursue my aspirations.

Despite my years of experience supporting others, I find myself amid an intensely personal battle with grief. It's a search for answers that linger just beyond reach, a yearning for peace that often feels elusive. My professional background hasn't shielded me from the deep emotional weight of this process, reminding me that grief is an individual journey unique to each person.

Grief is not a straight path; it's full of unexpected turns. Healing doesn't mean moving forward in a linear way but unfolding over time, sometimes slowly and with effort. I've learned that this is true for myself and the people I support.

Choosing to include "therapist" in the book's title was intentional. It highlights the professional lens I bring to this topic while acknowledging that I, too, am on this therapeutic journey. My own experiences are interwoven with the lessons I aim to share, showing that even those who study grief struggle with its emotional weight. This universality is what I hope to convey—grief transcends expertise and speaks to the human condition.

Embracing grief has grown into something more significant than a personal journey. It's a calling I'm fully embracing as I continue to work with others grieving their own losses. My brother's absence remains intertwined with my life. However, the mourning and healing process has become both a reflection of my inner landscape and a testament to resilience.

Looking back, I see the progress I've made in coming to terms with his loss. Acceptance is a work in progress, but it reminds me that grief never truly ends—it evolves. The pages of this book reflect that journey, a reminder that grief, while challenging, can transform into a force that propels us forward and allows us to embrace the bittersweet beauty of life.

TABLE OF CONTENTS

CHAPTER 1
BOUND BEYOND BLOOD

He has always been, and remains to this day, my best friend—the one constant presence in my life since I was just three years old. The memory of his arrival is etched in my mind like a vivid snapshot, one I can quickly summon whenever I think back to those early days. I can still see myself as a wide-eyed toddler, curiosity brimming as I peered into his cozy crib, trying to comprehend this tiny, new life that would soon become such a fundamental part of my world.

Somewhere in the depths of my basement, tucked away in a forgotten box, lie remnants of that particular time—baby blankets that my aunt had gifted my mother on a particularly chilly night during a long drive from Fords, NJ, to Staten Island, NY. At the time, those blankets felt like a soft, warm embrace, wrapping me in their comforting texture. As I think back now, their rough material—woven from horsehair—seems far less inviting. Yet, they hold a more profound significance beyond their feel; they represent the cocoon of safety and warmth that surrounded me in those early years.

These blankets, though rougher now in memory, are more than just pieces of fabric. They are symbols of a time when life was simple, when the world was filled with the innocence of childhood, and when my friendship with him was beginning to take root—a friendship that would grow into one of the

1

most meaningful relationships of my life.

He wasn't just my first cousin, but he was a unique and intricate familial bond that connected us through both sides of our family tree. This rare connection stemmed from a brother and sister from one family marrying a brother and sister from another, creating an unusually intertwined web of relationships that shaped the very fabric of our lives. Growing up amid these complex family dynamics, we often found ourselves acting more like siblings despite each having older brothers. While we shared the same DNA, our bond evolved into something far deeper than blood as we transitioned into adulthood.

It became increasingly evident that our connection transcended the label of cousinhood. We shared experiences, emotions, and a mutual understanding that surpassed the relationships we had with our own siblings. This growing awareness brought us even closer. We became each other's confidants, relying on one another for support, comfort, and companionship. What began as a familial bond blossomed into a brother-sister *relationship*, fortified by years of shared laughter, struggles, and milestones.

In essence, we weren't just cousins — we became siblings in the truest sense, bound not only by family ties but by a profound connection of the heart and spirit. It was a lifelong bond that weathered the tests of time and circumstance, proving stronger with each passing year.

He was always by my side, and I treasure the countless pictures that capture the moments we shared. Back then, when photography wasn't as ubiquitous as it is now, the few snapshots from my childhood stood out vividly in my memory. What's remarkable is that most of these cherished images feature Lou rather than my siblings from my family of origin. These photos preserve memories of birthday parties filled with laughter, my first communion, and those awkward pre-teen moments we all go through. It's funny to think that our bond only deepened over time despite the absence of modern conveniences — no cell phones, cordless phones, or the internet.

Lou wasn't just *like* a brother; he was my confidant, my closest friend, the one with whom I shared countless adventures — both grand and small. Whether it was something as ordinary as a walk in the park or a significant milestone, I always looked forward to our time together. Each interaction strengthened our relationship and our friendship, solidifying a bond that felt unbreakable.

Even now, after his passing, the weight of our connection remains — profound and ever-present. The memories we created are my anchor, a wellspring of strength and comfort that I return to time and again. They serve as a constant reminder of the enduring love and companionship we share. These experiences didn't just define our relationship; they shaped who I am today. They continue to offer solace during my most difficult moments, a testament to the lasting imprint that meaningful connections leave on our hearts and lives.

The impact of his presence is as real today as it was when he was here, a timeless influence that continues to shape and guide me.

Lou and his beloved dog, Collie Zack, in 1995.

CHAPTER 2
SILENT SOLACE

It's not uncommon for any of us to reflect on past experiences, especially in the aftermath of losing a loved one. This tendency is a natural response to grief; the mind revisits key moments and interactions, sifting through them for any signs of missteps or missed opportunities. We often replay events in our minds, wondering about the things we could have done differently or better. One memory that will remain forever etched in my heart is the night Lou chose to stay with me — just hours before my mother passed away.

The specifics of that evening are somewhat blurred, and I can't quite recall where Lou spent the night. He may have found a place to rest at my grandmother's house. Yet, what stands out more than the details is the overwhelming sense of isolation I felt at the time. My boyfriend, now my husband, had gone home earlier, leaving me alone with my thoughts and the weight of impending loss. When Lou arrived late that night, his presence was like a quiet, steadying force that I desperately needed in my deepening sadness.

We spent hours together sifting through old photographs. This activity might seem mundane to some, but it was, at least for me, a lifeline. There weren't many pictures of us, but a significant portion of the collection dated back to the World War II era, sparking a flood of nostalgic stories and memories.

As we shared these moments, Lou became more than just a comforting presence — he became a bridge between the past and present, offering me a form of solace that transcended the ordinary.

His ability to truly listen and be there for me during such a turbulent time forged a strong bond. The comfort he provided wasn't temporary; it wove itself into the fabric of my being as the reality of my loss unfolded. That kind of comfort felt during moments of deep grief transforms into a sacred memory. This cherished connection lingers long after a loved one is gone. This shared experience of support and understanding becomes a lasting refuge, a memory we tightly clutch as we navigate the unpredictable waves of emotion that follow loss.

In those quiet hours with Lou, as we leafed through the remnants of the past, he gave me more than companionship. He gave me the strength to face my grief and the knowledge that, even amid sorrow, the bond we shared would continue to offer solace — a refuge in my heart that would endure for years to come.

CHAPTER 3
WHY IS THIS HAPPENING?

The period during which he first confided in me about his illness felt almost surreal, as though I was moving through life on autopilot—barely able to comprehend the enormity of what was unfolding. It was a strange time, where reality seemed to blur with the tangled web of my thoughts and emotions, casting an ever-present shadow over what used to feel like a normal existence. Despite the physical distance that grew between us when he relocated to the East Coast, we somehow managed to sustain—if not deepen—our connection. We found ways to communicate more frequently than we ever had before, making our early morning phone calls and text messages an almost sacred routine. Both of us, by then, had developed the habit of waking up early, often arriving at our respective workplaces a good 90 minutes before the actual start of the workday. It was our time—a slice of normalcy in a world that was rapidly becoming anything but.

Then came the turning point—when his health took a devastating nosedive. The pain, which had once been intermittent, became a constant, unwelcome companion in his life. It was no longer something that ebbed and flowed—it just *was* seeping into every facet of his daily existence. Each new update on his condition hit me like a wave, bringing with it a fresh surge of fear and uncertainty. Yet, amid the storm of emotions, I found a strange, unexpected comfort—one I didn't know I needed or could rely on. The unwavering support of those around me became a lifeline: my friends, colleagues from the office, long-forgotten high school acquaintances who resurfaced just when I needed them, neighbors who had quietly woven themselves into the fabric of my daily life, my closest friend, and most importantly, my daughters.

This collective web of support formed a kind of emotional cushion—softening the sharp edges of the fear and helplessness we were both feeling. It was as though, in his suffering, I had stumbled upon an unlikely sanctuary built not from solitude but from the love and care of those around me.

The entire ordeal wasn't just an emotional drain—it was a profound test of endurance, both physically exhausting and deeply terrifying. Coming to terms with the stark reality of his cancer diagnosis felt like our lives had been shaken to their core, the foundation beneath us crumbling as we were forced to confront some of life's harshest truths: the fragility of health, the looming shadow of mortality, and the sheer unpredictability that life holds. Every day wasn't just a mental hurdle—it *was* a fresh challenge, each one unique in its own way, demanding more than the last. I found myself struggling to navigate my own tangled emotions while, at the same time, trying to be a pillar of strength for him. It was an incredibly tough period where the weight of responsibility, fear, and love collided, leaving little room for anything else.

Seven years have now passed since I lost him—a loss that unfolded amidst a whirlwind of events so sudden and chaotic that they still feel unreal. It all transpired over the painfully short span of four months, a time that, looking back, feels like both an eternity and the blink of an eye.

At first, things seemed relatively normal—deceptively so. It all began with a string of troubling phone calls, subtle hints that something wasn't quite right. He mentioned a visit to the doctor and some vague complaints about pain. But every time, he gave me reassurances—brushed off my concerns in the way he had, always trying to downplay the severity of things as if to protect me from the worst. Initially, the doctors echoed his calm demeanor, assuring us that there was no real cause for alarm. We were told that these were likely minor health issues—nothing more than a temporary setback.

But those reassurances, though comforting for a brief moment, soon began to unravel. The veneer of normalcy we clung to was shattered by the harsh reality that followed, a reality far more devastating than either of us could have imagined.

I was always scared in the back of my mind—though I tried to suppress it. I knew that Lou was a heavy smoker, and deep down, I feared the inevitable consequences. It wasn't long before those fears materialized into something far worse than I had imagined. The life-altering news came: a cancer diagnosis that sent shockwaves through our lives, flipping my world upside down in an instant. The very mention of *cancer* left me numb, struggling to comprehend the weight of what lay ahead. My initial disbelief quickly transformed into a whirlwind of activity—listening to discussions about medical appointments, treatment plans, and prognosis. We were plunged into the murky depths of uncertainty, trying to make sense of a situation that defied explanation.

He would undergo chemotherapy, followed by surgery—a daunting and formidable treatment regimen that we all hoped would be the miracle we desperately needed. But as the days passed, it became clear that hope wasn't enough. The side effects were brutal, a relentless assault on his body, and despite our collective determination, the treatment didn't deliver the results we had longed for. The weight of that realization hit hard—there was no miracle cure, no easy way out.

In a last-ditch effort to cling to any remaining hope, we turned to immunotherapy, a treatment that offered a glimmer of possibility. The prospect of a new approach gave us a momentary reprieve, a fleeting belief that maybe, just maybe, this could turn the tide. For a short while, it felt like we had a lifeline—one that could alter the course of his illness. But even the promise of modern medicine, with all its advancements, ultimately fell short.

Each day became a battleground of emotions as we were forced to confront the stark reality of his declining health. The emotional toll was immense—an exhausting push and pull between hope and despair. We found ourselves living in the shadow of an impending loss, one that loomed ever closer, darkening our days and leaving us to grapple with the knowledge that time was slipping away faster than we could grasp.

CHAPTER 4
COUNTING HOPES

I started driving from New York to Cincinnati regularly, a journey that soon became routine but was marked by a kind of chaotic urgency that, in hindsight, felt almost psychotic. The drive itself was a reflection of the mental state I was in — racing against time and fear. In fact, the sheer anxiety I experienced might inspire another book, this one about the profound dread that flying induces in some of us. My first trip down occurred in April, not long after he received his initial diagnosis.

When I first got the call and learned about his diagnosis — bladder cancer, specifically — it didn't hit me with the overwhelming wave of dread that I had always imagined it would. Yes, the news was incredibly tough, and the fear was very real. However, there was also a flicker of something else inside me — determination, perhaps. I knew right away that I had to inform my family. Although the burden of delivering that news weighed heavily on my heart, I held fast to the belief that we could overcome this. With enough motivation and some creative thinking, I told myself we might just conquer this together.

When I spoke to him, I promised I'd be there for his first chemotherapy session, a vow that felt important — both to him and to me. Almost immediately, I set my plans into motion. I arranged to take a week off from work, making it possible for me to drive down to Cincinnati. The trip was long, but I didn't make it alone; I traveled with his father-in-law, both of us bracing ourselves for what lay ahead. The car was filled with an unspoken tension, a quiet yet palpable sense of solidarity as we prepared to confront the beginning of his treatment.

Reflecting on my previous summer trip to Cincinnati with two of my daughters, I remembered how he had just moved there. It wasn't unusual for him—he was always someone who didn't stay rooted in one place for too long, having lived in various parts of the country throughout his adult life. His restlessness contrasted sharply with my own stable existence. I had hardly moved at all, certainly not across states or to different regions. In fact, the idea of such a cross-country trek always seemed daunting to me, so the thought of driving to Cincinnati with his father-in-law made me a bit nervous.

Yet, as it turned out, my anxiety about the drive quickly faded. We bonded almost immediately, united by our shared concern for him and his wife. Despite the gravity of the situation, there was something oddly comforting about having someone by my side who understood the weight of it all without needing to say much. The journey was long, stretching across highways that seemed to blur together after hours on the road. But there was a subtle importance in keeping ourselves occupied, even distracted, as the miles rolled by.

To pass the time, we began counting roadkill—a morbid yet strangely amusing game—and engaged in light-hearted banter. It gave us a way to cope with the surreal nature of what was happening. I found myself fluctuating between concern and cautious hope. My mind was filled with memories of my own mother, who I had lost to that same cruel illness years earlier. I could still vividly recall the toll it had taken on her, and that memory haunted me during the drive. But, despite everything, I clung to the belief that maybe, just maybe, things could turn out differently this time. That hope, fragile as it was, kept me going—kept me from sinking into despair.

In my quest for additional treatment options, I immersed myself in research, eager to uncover any advancements that could offer him even the slightest fighting chance. I discovered several promising possibilities, including radio wave therapies in Cleveland, which immediately caught my attention and sparked a glimmer of hope. Beyond conventional medicine, I also explored alternative paths, delving into the healing properties of crystals. I carefully selected a set to send to him, each one chosen with intention. One crystal, in particular, stood out to me—its shape, eerily resembling a bladder, gave the gesture a more profound sense of meaning and purpose. I even began reading books about faith healing, searching for anything that could make a difference.

In hindsight, it seems to me that there should be one more stage added to the famous model of Death and Dying—*desperation*. That's where I found myself—reaching out to everyone I knew, asking for prayers, regardless of their religious backgrounds or beliefs. I wanted to cover every possible base, leaving no stone unturned in this battle against his illness. Losing my brother wasn't an option in my mind; I was resolute and fiercely committed to fighting alongside him in whatever way I could, no matter how unconventional.

I'm sure many of you have found yourselves in similar situations—driven by a sense of desperation, willing to try anything in the hope of changing the outcome.

CHAPTER 5
STARK CONTRASTS

The drive underscored the striking contrasts within the country, starting with the bustling urban sprawl of New York City before transitioning into New Jersey's more industrialized outskirts. As we progressed, the urban landscape gradually gave way to county highways, where enormous billboards dotted the roadside, advertising local attractions and an eclectic array of goods. These signs tantalized travelers with options for breakfast stops, opportunities to purchase fireworks, or even offers to buy firearms. Some exits along the route beckoned with promises of intriguing destinations, such as caves awaiting exploration—tempting diversions on an otherwise long drive.

As the journey continued, the scenery transformed even more dramatically. The urban energy faded into amusement parks and roadside attractions, a vibrant counterpoint to the long, unbroken stretches of highway that characterized Pennsylvania. The roads wound through hilly terrain, cutting through tunnels carved into the mountains, adding an undeniable sense of adventure to the trip. For me, the sight of high bridges always stirs a certain unease—and it seems that navigating through mountainous terrain triggers a similar apprehension.

Yet, despite the challenges, the entire experience reinforced just how diverse the American landscape truly is. From the dynamic pulse of urban life to the rugged beauty of rural expanses, all of it was encapsulated within this single, sweeping journey across state lines—a reminder of the country's vastness and its endless variety.

I had taken a trip to Pennsylvania once before to visit a friend I had met through Yahoo groups. She lived near Shanksville, a small town forever etched into history because of the tragic events surrounding Flight 93. Having spent much of my life in New York City, I felt an undeniable pull to pay my respects to the heroes of that flight, whose incredible courage had left an indelible mark on all of us. The journey took me through the rolling hills of Pennsylvania. As I drove, I reflected on the significance of honoring those who had made the ultimate sacrifice that fateful day.

| Up until that point, the furthest I had ever driven was to that part of Pennsylvania, a region steeped in natural beauty and historical weight. When I finally arrived at my friend's home, the experience was as poignant as it was eye-opening. Just a couple of exits further down the highway, a simple turn south transported me into an entirely different environment—one filled with unique landscapes and rural charm, a stark contrast to the urban intensity of New York City. Each mile felt like a passage through different worlds as the landscape unfolded to reveal the rich tapestry of life beyond the city limits.

That trip left a lasting impression on me, not only because of the deep history connected to Shanksville but also because it was my first real glimpse into how dramatically different life could be just a few hours away from the city I knew so well.

CHAPTER 6
FLASHBACKS AND URGENCY

The time spent driving through West Virginia felt fleeting, almost surreal—like passing through a dream you can't quite grasp. The stretch of the state we traversed wasn't the picturesque landscape of rolling blue hills that West Virginia is so often celebrated for. Instead, our view was dominated by sprawling industrial complexes and a seemingly endless parade of billboards. These signs promised everything from the "best dinner in town" to fireworks and firearms for sale—an unexpected and rather commercial side of the state that caught me a bit off guard.

As we crossed a small bridge, we quietly transitioned into Ohio. The shift was subtle yet unmistakable, marking a new chapter in our journey. The scenery changed, and with it, the mood—though my mind remained in a state of quiet contemplation. Sleep, throughout this trip, was a rare luxury. I found myself wide awake, not wanting to show any signs of weariness or disrespect to my host and driver. Their hospitality meant a great deal to me, so I kept my fatigue and racing thoughts to myself, choosing instead to remain silent for most of the ride.

In those moments of silence, I often turned inward, engaging in desperate prayers that only seem to emerge when life presents you with heavy, uncertain circumstances. Each prayer was laced with hope, fear, and a kind of urgency that only deepened as the miles ticked by.

I recalled an instructor from my past who once shared a profound insight: during times of crisis, people often revert to the prayers of their childhood. That simple truth resonated deeply with me, especially in moments like this. As we drove along the highway, my mind drifted back to the many prayers the nuns had taught me in Catholic school. Each mantra, each supplication, returned with clarity—like old friends from a distant time, bringing with them a comforting sense of familiarity. It was remarkable how those simple, well-worn phrases could provide such solace, grounding me amidst the uncertainty of our journey. They connected me to a faith and a period of my life that felt both distant and immediate, especially when faced with challenges like these.

As we passed through Columbus, the familiar question that echoes in every long road trip surfaced in my mind: "Are we there yet?" It was the sort of phrase that could have easily come from the backseat of a car, embodying the restless energy of a seven-year-old eager to reach their destination. But this time, it echoed in my own thoughts as I quietly willed the miles to pass more quickly. After weaving through the hustle and bustle of the city, the scenery shifted dramatically once more. The urban sprawl faded, replaced by open fields and stretches of quiet, rural roads. With each mile, I wasn't just counting the distance—we were getting closer to his home, and I could feel the tension growing in my chest.

A sense of urgency gripped me. There was an unspoken pressure, a knot of anxiety in my stomach, as I focused intently on the road ahead. Every minute seemed to stretch longer, weighed down by the anticipation of what awaited us.

The countdown to our arrival became more than just a measure of time—it was the thin line separating hope from despair.

Anita and Lou in Grandma's House in 1967.

CHAPTER 7
A PILGRIMAGE OF SORTS

I hadn't yet mentioned that this journey was unfolding on *Good Friday*—a day laden with deep, somber significance in the Christian calendar. Typically, I would spend this time in quiet reflection and retreat, often in Vermont, where I could contemplate and pray. But this year was markedly different, the solemnity of the day heightened by the gravity of our journey. The trip was steeped in sadness—layered with dual emotions that pulled at my heart in ways I hadn't anticipated. On the one hand, there was the inherent sorrow of *why* we were traveling: the relentless weight of his illness and the uncertainty it cast over our lives. On the other hand, profound grief naturally accompanied Good Friday, a day of remembrance of suffering and sacrifice.

It felt like the gravity of the day itself—laden with mourning and reflection—had settled over me like a thick, unshakable fog. Yet, even in the midst of that sorrow, there was a flicker of hope. I carried with me a quiet, prayerful wish that he might somehow overcome the challenges posed by his bladder cancer. Every mile we drove seemed to be a poignant reminder of the delicate balance between despair and optimism. The tension between these two emotions was palpable, as if the air was charged with fear and possibility.

As the journey continued, this emotional push and pull

deepened, creating a heavy and hopeful atmosphere — almost like the very essence of Good Friday itself. It mirrored the complexities of the moment we were living in a time of grief, yes, but also a time where hope still lingered, fragile but present. Each passing mile became a meditation on this strange juxtaposition, a reflection of the delicate realities we were forced to confront. The day's sorrow blended with my private grief, but somehow, a small part of me still clung to the belief that, despite everything, he might yet find a way to defy the odds.

It was a strange and poignant journey, one that felt almost like a pilgrimage of sorts. Not just to see him but to confront the swirling emotions that came with the uncertainty of his illness — and with life itself. In the quiet moments of the drive, I reflected deeply, considering the intertwining forces of faith, fear, and hope. Like the roads we traveled, all of them stretched endlessly ahead, with no clear destination in sight.

CHAPTER 8
KEEPING PRESENT

When we finally arrived at his home, I honestly can't recall who greeted us at the door. The faces blur in my memory, but what remains crystal clear is the warmth of the hugs that followed—those embraces filling the space between us with a sense of comfort, familiarity, and a shared understanding of what lay ahead. I was genuinely glad to be there, not just as a visitor but as someone who could hopefully offer him much-needed encouragement. The thought of being a source of strength for him, someone who might inspire him to keep fighting through his struggles, gave me purpose in the midst of uncertainty. I spent an entire week there, which was unusual for me; I don't think I've ever stayed in someone else's home for that long before. Typically, I'm quick to retreat to my own space, but this time was different—this time, it felt necessary to stay, to immerse myself in his world for a little while.

During my stay, I found moments of levity and laughter, especially when I discovered his unexpected fondness for car chase movies. They weren't exactly my go-to choose for entertainment, but I couldn't help but appreciate how animated he got while watching them. There was something almost childlike about the way he'd lean forward, completely absorbed in the action. It brought a lightness to the room that was otherwise filled with the weight of his illness. Even though car chases weren't really my cup of tea, I couldn't help but laugh along with him, finding joy in his enthusiasm. Each morning, we'd sit together and enjoy strong black coffee—something that had always been a staple in my life. It became part of our routine during that week, a small ritual that felt grounding amidst all the uncertainty.

Then came Easter Sunday—a day with its own layers of significance. His wife and father-in-law headed off to church, inviting me to join them. He encouraged me to go along, but something inside me resisted. There was an inexplicable pull to stay behind, to spend that day with him, even if it meant doing nothing more than sitting quietly together. At the same time, the television blared some mindless show in the background. Maybe, deep down, there was an instinct that told me this would be our last time together. I can't say for sure, but I know I felt it—that strong sense that I needed to be there with him in that moment for reasons I couldn't fully explain at the time.

Looking back, I realize that Easter Sunday turned out to be one of my life's most meaningful and cherished experiences. It wasn't filled with grand gestures or deep conversations but rather the simple act of *being*—sharing space, sharing time, and connecting in a way that transcended the noise of illness and uncertainty. In the small, seemingly insignificant moments, I found the essence of genuine connection. In hindsight, that quiet afternoon together symbolizes the heart of what matters—being present, even when there's nothing to say, and finding comfort in the simple, shared act of just being with someone you love.

CHAPTER 9
BEING AN ANCHOR

The following morning unfolded with a palpable sense of heaviness. My brother, along with his wife father-in-law, and I, made our way to the chemotherapy center, leaving behind a silence that weighed heavily on my heart. The gravity of the situation loomed over me like a dark cloud, casting an unshakable shadow over everything. In the midst of this emotional storm, I couldn't recall whether I had managed to say a prayer or simply sat frozen in silence. What I remember most vividly was the overwhelming disbelief that we had found ourselves in this cruel reality—facing a battle we never imagined we'd have to fight. The thought of my brother undergoing a treatment fraught with such uncertainty and fear was almost too much to bear, and it all felt surreal.

Despite this sense of helplessness, I knew how important it was to maintain a positive mindset in the face of such adversity. It wasn't just for him—it was for me, for all of us who loved him and wanted to see him come through this. I realized that to be the support he needed; I had to focus my energy on hope and encouragement, even though the fear of the unknown was gnawing at me. The challenge was in balancing that fear with determination.

To help him through the ordeal, I threw myself into research. I started reading everything I could about chemotherapy and the side effects that would inevitably accompany it. My aim was to equip myself with knowledge — hoping that if I understood what lay ahead, I could offer him some semblance of comfort or relief. I scoured the internet, looking for tips, remedies, and practical strategies to combat the nausea, fatigue, and other grueling effects that so often accompany the treatment. From alternative therapies to nutrition tips, I immersed myself in anything that could make his journey even a bit easier.

What struck me most during this process was the sheer volume of information — some hopeful, some daunting — but all of it reinforced the importance of being prepared. I began compiling lists of ideas: herbal teas to soothe the stomach, stretches to help with the inevitable fatigue and even recipes for meals that might appeal to his changing appetite. It was a small way for me to feel in control, to feel like I could still do something — anything — to help.

I sought inspiration through literature that chronicled miraculous recoveries, searching for books that not only could uplift his spirits but also instill within him a sense of resilience and the belief that recovery was possible. It wasn't enough to be there for him; I needed him to know — deep down — that he wasn't fighting this battle alone. Stories of triumph existed, and I wanted him to see that he, too, could be one of those stories. These books became a lifeline, a way to connect him to the hope that felt so fragile in the face of his illness.

I became deeply fascinated with the concept of visualization as a tool in the fight against cancer. The idea that mental imagery could influence the body's healing process captured my attention, and I dove into researching techniques that could help him envision a brighter, healthier future. I read everything I could about how visualization might aid recovery—how picturing the body healing itself could bring about real change or, at the very least, bolster the spirit.

It felt imperative to gather these resources and insights, building a comprehensive support system that could strengthen his emotional and mental resilience. In this moment of overwhelming uncertainty, I was determined to be a source of unwavering strength and positivity for him. I wanted to do everything in my power to uplift him—mentally, emotionally, and spiritually. *If* I could provide him with the tools to imagine his own healing, then maybe I could help him feel empowered, even when the reality of his situation felt bleak.

In those days, my role shifted. I wasn't just a sister or a companion in his struggle—I became a quiet architect, piecing together any form of support that might give him even a sliver of hope. It was all I could do, but it was everything I had.

CHAPTER 10
SHOCK

As the situation worsened, I found myself returning to June over and over, each visit more heart-wrenching than the last, as I became painfully aware that the outcome was likely bleak. After my initial visit following the diagnosis, I made another trip—but this time, I wasn't alone. My middle daughter chose to accompany me, and her presence became a comforting balm on what was quickly becoming an increasingly long and emotionally arduous journey. As we traversed the distance, the hours seemed to stretch endlessly, and with each passing mile, my anxiety deepened. The weight of the situation pressed heavily on my mind, but I drew solace from her quiet support.

A specific moment during the drive still stands out—a text conversation we shared with him. His words, marked by the way he signed his last name, fluctuated wildly between erratic bursts of anger and moments of confusion. I could feel the emotional chaos he was going through. In that instant, an unsettling realization washed over me: *I was losing him*. The person I had known, the one with whom I shared so much history, was slipping away, and I was powerless to stop it.

When we finally arrived, the sight that greeted me was nothing short of shocking. His physical decline was stark and impossible to ignore. He had taken to using a walker, a stark symbol of his frailty, and his once-full cheeks had hollowed out, leaving him gaunt—a shell of the person I had seen just weeks earlier. The transformation was so drastic that I struggled to comprehend it, my heart breaking at the sight.

Yet, amid the heaviness of that moment, there was a flicker of gratitude for something small but meaningful. I had brought with me a picture book, one I had painstakingly crafted, filled with family photos that captured the joy and love we had shared over the years. My original intention was to give him it as a Christmas gift, a token of our bond. But standing there, it became painfully clear that time had shifted under our feet—that moment, which I had so carefully planned, had come too late. What had once been a gift for the future now felt like a relic of the past?

Throughout my life, I have always prided myself on my strong faith, finding comfort in my spiritual convictions. But in that moment, as I stood there facing the harsh reality of his deterioration, I found myself wrestling with God in a way I never had before. I silently but firmly declared that we were no longer on speaking terms. The weight of the circumstances overwhelmed me, and I felt consumed by a profound sense of isolation. It was as if the very foundation of my faith had been shaken, leaving me adrift in the midst of my distress—unsure of where to turn next and feeling utterly alone in my grief.

CHAPTER 11
WHY

The last time I made this trip was during the final weekend of his life.

Typically, the drive takes about 13 hours — a journey I had already made four times in the span of just four months. However, this particular trip felt markedly different from the others. For the first time, I chose to drive overnight. He was in the hospital now, no longer able to manage at home, and the doctors were transitioning him into hospice care. My purpose for traveling to Cincinnati this time was clear: to offer support not only to him but also to my new sister-in-law, who was enduring her own harrowing ordeal.

Despite the gravity of the situation, the drive felt surprisingly nonchalant, almost routine. Yet beneath that calm exterior, I carried a quiet determination. I clung to the belief that the end wasn't quite imminent — that there was still time. My heart held onto the hope that I'd return in a few weeks, perhaps with my oldest daughter, who was also his goddaughter, or maybe with my close friend and neighbor. I imagined a scenario where I'd have the chance to offer a more extended, heartfelt farewell — a bittersweet visit, yes, but one that would allow for more time.

Even as the underlying sadness crept in, I allowed myself to envision a future visit where things felt less than final. It was a fragile kind of hope, but one I needed to carry with me during that long, lonely drive. After all, hope, even the tiniest glimmer, had been my constant companion throughout this journey, and on this particular trip, I wasn't ready to let go of it just yet.

During this trip, I stayed at a modest motel — not luxurious by any means, but it served its purpose well enough. It reminded me of a budget Motel 6, where you don't expect frills, but it's comfortable for a short stay. The staff welcomed me warmly, their friendliness a small comfort during my brief eight-hour rest before returning to the road. My destination was the hospital in Cincinnati. I spoke with my sister-in-law over the phone that evening, and what she revealed left me shaken. The situation was far more dire than I had realized, forcing me to confront an unsettling question: *What do I tell my daughters?* How much should I share with them about the gravity of what was unfolding?

This dilemma weighed heavily on my mind, and even at that moment, I struggled to comprehend just how rapidly things would progress. The truth felt slippery, and the uncertainty gnawed at me as I tried to make sense of it all.

After a quick breakfast, I climbed back into my little car and resumed my journey — one that would take me through the winding roads of West Virginia and into Ohio.

There's a particular stretch of highway that stands out in my memory, a part of the trip I keep coming back to in my thoughts. It's a place where the road dips beneath an incredibly tall walkway bridge, an impressive arch that spans over the highway. For reasons I can't fully explain, this bridge has etched itself into my mind, almost becoming a symbol of the entire journey.

It's strange how something so seemingly ordinary—a fleeting moment on the road—can embed itself in your memory, resurfacing long after the experience has passed. I've even seen it in my dreams, this towering archway looming over me. I can only wonder what someone versed in dream interpretation might say about such an image and how a simple piece of infrastructure can carry so much weight in the subconscious.

The road, the bridge, and that inexplicable feeling of foreboding all came together in a way I didn't quite understand then—but looking back, it seems almost prophetic. It was as if, even before I reached the hospital, part of me already knew the gravity of what lay ahead.

CHAPTER 12
INEVITABILITY

The drive itself wasn't particularly long—just about four hours at most. Soon enough, I found myself pulling up to the hospital in Cincinnati. The building was imposing—massive and teeming with activity, with a constant flow of people entering and leaving. As I stepped into the lobby, the soothing sound of a piano filled the air, creating an odd sense of calm amidst the usual chaos of hospital life. It was a slight reprieve, a moment of tranquility that seemed almost out of place but was deeply appreciated as I prepared myself for what lay ahead.

Navigating my way up to the floor where my relative was staying, I steeled myself for the inevitable emotions that would come. Once there, I immediately let my sister-in-law take a break—she needed to go home, shower, and rest, which she had barely done in days. I settled into the room with him, ready to support him through whatever came next. For the first time, we had a candid conversation about the severity of his condition, something that had been looming but left unsaid for too long. I was a social worker, well-versed in handling sensitive topics, yet surprisingly, it wasn't me who broached the subject.

It was he who initiated the conversation. "You know, sis, this is it," he said, his voice calm but filled with a heaviness that hung in the air. I was momentarily stunned, left searching for the right words—something meaningful, something that could match the gravity of what he was saying. Instead, what came out felt inadequate, almost trivial.

"I know," I managed to stammer, "but as long as your mind doesn't want it to be..." The words felt hollow as if I was grasping for something deeper but failing to express it. I wished, desperately, that I could have offered more, that I could have found some way to comfort him with something profound or meaningful at that moment.

I beat myself up for it—over and over again. The feeling of inadequacy haunted me as I sat there, wishing I had said or done something more. The silence between us grew, and I felt the weight of my missed opportunity hanging heavy in the room.

But I reassured him in the best way I knew how. I told him we loved him—how much he meant to me and how much my three daughters adored him. I gently touched his shoulder, trying to communicate the love and support I struggled to put into words. I promised him I would be there for him, no matter what.

As I finally sank into the soft bench in the corner of the room, I couldn't help but chastise myself for not being more straightforward, for not saying what I should have. The realization hit me hard—this kind of emotional honesty isn't something you can learn in graduate school or through any formal training. Life's most significant moments often catch us completely off guard, leaving us fumbling for the right words when we need them the most. And despite everything I thought I knew, I was just as lost in that moment as anyone would be, grappling with the rawness of the situation and my own inadequacies in dealing with it.

At a specific moment, when he seemed momentarily aware of his surroundings—though I can't pinpoint exactly when it happened—we found ourselves engaged in a conversation about his toys. This discussion stirred a deep sense of nostalgia within me, especially given my own childhood experiences. My parents were never particularly keen on buying the latest or most sought-after toys. Instead, I often ended up with knock-offs that lacked the quality and authenticity of what many of my friends had. The contrast between what I owned and what he had was stark—his toys were always superior, closer to what children typically coveted. It was a small but significant reminder of how different our upbringings had been, though we rarely dwelled on such things.

Later that day, I shared a quick dinner with my sister-in-law and her father at a local barbecue restaurant. The Midwest has a well-earned reputation for doing barbecue exceptionally well, and that evening certainly lived up to it. Dining in that roadhouse establishment offered a brief and welcome respite from the emotional weight that had brought me to his home. After dinner, I stayed overnight at his place. Hospice care was being arranged to be provided at home, and we spent part of the evening discussing small logistics—like which television would be best suited for the bedroom. It was a small, almost trivial detail, especially when compared to the larger, more pressing realities we were all facing.

The plan had been for me to stay through the weekend, hoping to remain until he was stable enough to return home. But during the night, things took an unexpected and devastating turn. He deteriorated quickly, and I received a call from my sister-in-law informing me that he would need to be moved to a medical hospice facility. It was a moment that felt hauntingly familiar. In 1977, when my mother passed away, I had been through something eerily similar. The memories of that time came rushing back with clarity, and I recognized all too well the signs that the end was near.

CHAPTER 13
KINDNESS OF STRANGERS

At the hospital on Saturday, I learned more about the fact that the medical team had decided to transition him into hospice care. From that point forward, everything began to move incredibly fast. I quickly coordinated with my sister-in-law to establish a plan: I would return home rather than remain at the hospital, with the intention of flying back down on Wednesday. This return trip was crucial, as it would allow my oldest daughter the chance to say goodbye to her godfather—a moment I knew would be deeply important for both of them.

I vividly recall the phone call I made to my daughter, explaining the gravity of the situation. I described it as the *worst-case scenario*, a reality we were all struggling to come to terms with. Despite the heaviness of the conversation, I reassured her that I would come home to be with her and her siblings, and together, we would make the trip back. She needed to have the chance to express her love and say her farewells in person. As I spoke those words, a wave of realization hit me—an unshakable feeling that I might never see him again.

At that moment, my priorities became crystal clear: I needed to be at home with my girls to prepare them—and myself—for the inevitable news. As I wrestled with the emotional weight of the situation, I felt a strange sense of his spirit guiding me, urging me toward where I needed to be. It was as if he was releasing me from focusing solely on his condition, encouraging me to be present for my family.

At that point, I was filled with an overwhelming need to express my love and support, not just through my actions but through my words. I can't remember if he was conscious enough to understand or if he was able to respond, but I leaned in close and kissed his shoulder. I hoped, in some small way, that the gesture brought him comfort. I told him he was loved, hoping that — if nothing else — those words would reach him in some way, providing him with a measure of peace.

In the midst of this heart-wrenching experience, I embraced my sister-in-law tightly, our shared grief forming an unspoken bond that connected us in a way words never could. The sorrow that enveloped us was palpable, a collective weight that seemed to hang in the air. Yet, amidst the pain, I had a particularly poignant encounter with a nurse named Cheryl — at least, I believe that was her name — whose presence in that problematic environment was nothing short of remarkable. She worked tirelessly, navigating the emotional turbulence of her job with quiet grace and unwavering compassion.

When Cheryl wrapped her arms around me, it was more than just a gesture of comfort; it felt as though we had become family, united by the rawness of our shared experience. At that moment, her embrace was a lifeline — one I didn't know I needed until it was offered. There was a unique kind of strength in her empathy, an unspoken understanding that went beyond mere words. Her compassion infused me with a sense of solace I desperately craved in such a vulnerable time.

The memories of that weekend — the pain, the raw

emotions, and the surprising yet profound connections — remain etched in my mind, even now, all these years later. It's strange how moments of such intense sorrow can also bring forth the deepest human connections. Those fleeting encounters – like the one I shared with Cheryl - stand out as bright spots in the fog of grief, offering a reminder of the quiet power of empathy and the strength found in simply being present for one another.

CHAPTER 14
HOW DO I DO THIS?

I remember leaving the hospital — and driving back to New York to be with my girls as his life was slipping away. The weight of that moment still lingers in my mind, even now. As I prepared to leave, his father-in-law said, *"Godspeed."* That single word echoed through my thoughts the entire drive, like a mantra I couldn't shake. This was going to be a 13-hour solo journey, and I was in the most intense emotional state I had ever known. How was I supposed to manage this drive? The truth is, I didn't know if I could. I was completely unraveling — so much so that even attempting to talk on the phone was impossible. I couldn't focus on music, couldn't concentrate on anything at all. My mind was a fog of worry and grief, and all I had with me for the road were two bottles of water and a bag of pretzels.

How was I going to get through this?

The only thing I could do was pray.

How do you get through the last few hours of a loved one's life, especially when you are miles away — driving, no less? The helplessness is suffocating. I had to keep moving forward, knowing each mile brought me closer to the end yet farther from him. I gripped the steering wheel tighter, every muscle in my body tense as I tried to focus on the road ahead, but my thoughts were consumed by the unbearable truth I was trying to outrun.

I prayed—not just for strength, but for time. It was time to make it through the drive, be with him one last time, and hold on to whatever precious moments we had left. But deep down, I knew time wasn't on my side. That knowledge hung over me like a dark cloud, and yet I had no choice but to keep going.

How do you get through those final hours when you're on the road, isolated, and all you can do is count the minutes? The answer is you don't—you just *survive* them.

CHAPTER 15
BRILLIANCE AND SADNESS

It was one of those days when the sun seemed to shine brighter than usual, suspended in a clear blue sky that felt almost too perfect to be real. The warmth of summer was everywhere, wrapping itself around me like a familiar blanket, though I couldn't tell you the exact temperature at that moment. What I *did* know was that it was the kind of day made for being outside, basking in the vibrancy that hung in the air. I watched as cars streamed past, heading toward the amusement park nearby, the anticipation of thrills in the air. The rides were already in motion — spinning, twisting — set against a backdrop of cheerful screams and delighted laughter, all of it a world away from what I was feeling inside.

There was a rush of adrenaline in my veins as I drove, but it wasn't from excitement. No, this was different — a kind of restless energy mixed with a gnawing awareness of the need to stay within the speed limit. My mind kept replaying the same cautionary reminders about the consequences of speeding. The last thing I needed was to get pulled over, ticketed, or delayed by something as trivial as that.

I switched off my phone without a second thought, knowing that I couldn't handle any more distractions or interruptions. There was no space in my mind for calls or notifications that might further complicate an already fragile state of mind. At that moment, I was consumed by an overwhelming sense of sorrow—so heavy it rendered me unable to form any coherent words. All I could manage was a mournful, gut-wrenching wail, one that seemed to rise up from deep within me. It echoed through the quiet stillness of my thoughts, clashing violently with the bright, sunny world outside—an almost cruel juxtaposition to that *God-awful, beautiful* July day.

The contrast was sharp and painful as if the universe itself was mocking me with its radiant perfection while I struggled under the weight of my inner turmoil. Each passing second felt surreal, caught between the warmth of summer and the cold, hollow ache of loss that gnawed at my insides.

CHAPTER 16
MY EXHAUSTION

It's hard to truly grasp the vastness of the journey through Ohio and the stretch across Pennsylvania that follows. (There are a million or so songs written about driving to get home— each one seemingly inadequate to capture the emotion of the ride.) Ohio itself is remarkably flat, and as soon as you leave Columbus, the landscape transitions into miles upon miles of agricultural land. The scenery is dominated by fields that roll out like a vast green carpet, and along the highways, you can't help but notice the numerous billboards. Many of them carry messages urging travelers to remember the Ten Commandments or to reflect on various moral reminders— constant interruptions in the scenery. In a sense, they are always present, but rather than offering solace, they seem to heighten the sense of isolation during such a heavy moment.

If you're feeling exhausted, the drive can become even riskier. The monotony of the long, straight roads has a way of lulling you into a trance-like state, almost hypnotic, as you focus on the white lines marking the lanes. Being alone during such a time is incredibly challenging. I had no one to share the ride with, no one to break the silence that hung heavily in the air.

The music was blaring—filling the car with sound—a deliberate choice to drown out my own thoughts, which felt overwhelming. This reaction isn't unusual for someone who is grieving; the last thing you want is to face the thoughts swirling in your mind.

Besides the noise from the speakers, a deeper unease gnawed at me. How would I explain this devastating loss to my daughters? He was their only uncle, a crucial figure in their lives, and now he was gone. It's an impossible task to find ways to comfort others when you're struggling to find comfort within yourself. The tragedy had struck so suddenly, without warning or preparation, that it left me reeling—questioning everything I thought I understood about God and the world. I've always tried to be a good person—at least, I've made an effort to do right by others—but here I was, feeling utterly alone in my grief.

Now, I was losing the last connection to my childhood—the one person who understood our upbringing. He was the only one who could relate to the unique experience of having a grandmother who couldn't cook—an experience that was both comical and all too real for us. The laughter we once shared over it now felt distant, almost unreachable.

The first part of the drive passed in a blur, my mind racing in a thousand different directions, scowling at billboards that seemed out of place in my tumultuous state. Whenever I saw one imploring me to repent, it only deepened the feeling of despair. It was as if those signs were speaking to a part of me that was already fractured beyond repair. I felt as though I was already living in some form of hell.

Despite the miles I put behind me, the journey felt far from over, and it was hard to shake the weight of everything that had happened.

CHAPTER 17
IMMINENT LOSS

I mentioned the stages of death and dying earlier. The Kübler-Ross theory, widely recognized as the Stages of Grief, is highly respected and garners considerable attention in both clinical and popular contexts. These stages have become a *fundamental* aspect of grief counseling and are now a staple on licensing examinations for social workers and mental health professionals. Numerous books have been published that explore these stages in depth, reflecting their lasting significance in helping us understand the grieving process. I vividly recall first encountering these stages many years ago, but my personal experience with them began when I was just nineteen—following the devastating loss of my mother. The acronym DABDA, representing Denial, Anger, Bargaining, Depression, and Acceptance, served as a critical framework for processing that profound grief, guiding me through each phase.

Recently, my thoughts have gravitated back to these stages as I faced the imminent loss of my brother. The gravity of the situation—knowing we had mere hours, perhaps only minutes left—felt suffocating. I found myself in uncharted emotional territory. In this raw moment, I began questioning the relevance of bargaining. I felt far beyond that stage, wrestling instead with the stark reality of the situation, which offered little to no room for negotiation. It's led me to wonder whether, once this is over, I'll be left stuck in Anger and Depression—two stages that can linger, sometimes indefinitely, and profoundly alter one's experience of grief.

Reflecting on my family, particularly my daughters, I'm reminded of the challenges they faced just two years ago when we lost a dear friend. The impact on them was both immediate and profound. One moment, this beloved individual was present in their lives, vibrant and full of life — then suddenly, I had to explain that she was nearing the end. The abruptness of loss was a shock to their still-developing understanding of mortality. I recall their disbelief. "That can't be true," they insisted—desperate to deny the irreversible situation unfolding before them. Now, as I prepare to lose my brother, the thought of my daughters going through this heartbreaking experience again feels almost unbearable. The weight of history, compounded by the current loss, leaves me to navigate my own grief while also fearing for the emotional toll this will take on them.

We dealt with that loss as a family and will do the same this time, no matter how heavy the burden feels. Families, after all, aren't just bound by love but by shared sorrow, which, in time, may bring healing.

CHAPTER 18
TRANSFORMING MY
WORLD

Fear gripped me *tightly* as I drove, the speedometer climbing higher and higher with each passing moment, almost as if it were mocking my desperation. Hours had already slipped away, blending together, and the only thing I could focus on was the road ahead—pushing myself to stay sharp and to maintain *any* sense of attention. Occasionally, in my growing panic, I resorted to slapping my own face, a desperate attempt to jolt my senses back to the present as though physical pain could pierce through the fog of exhaustion. At one point, I screamed into the emptiness of the car, my voice echoing off the windows, filled with frustration, fear, and desperation that seemed to swallow me whole. I wasn't just shouting into the void; I was directing my anger upwards—towards God, towards Lou—names spilling from my lips in a chaotic mix of disbelief, sorrow, and rage. It felt as if the weight of all my emotions was crashing down at once, and the only response I could muster was to chant the word "focus" repeatedly, *desperately*, as if somehow that simple mantra could anchor me during this turbulent, never-ending journey.

Outside the vehicle, the world was transforming before my eyes as if mirroring the turmoil within me. The sun dipped lower on the horizon, casting long shadows and painting the sky in a shifting gradient. It started as a bright blue — calm, serene — but soon transitioned to a muted gray and finally gave way to deep shades of purple that signaled the day's inevitable end. Despite knowing this route as intimately as I knew my own skin, a knot of fear twisted deep inside my gut. I tried to push that worry aside, tried to tell myself it was irrational, but it pressed back harder — reminding me, insistently, that there were still miles to go. The landscape had shifted, too; I was surrounded by unfamiliar fields in Pennsylvania. The once-clear landmarks had blurred, becoming indistinguishable as I raced past them.

A question surged through my mind — a question that felt like it was tearing me apart from the inside out. *How could this be happening?* How could fate be so cruel, so unrelenting, as to take away the only family member I had left besides my children? Each bend in the road, each twist and turn, felt like a cruel reminder of the distance I still had to cover — both physically and emotionally — as I grappled with the growing, unbearable reality of what I was losing.

And what I didn't realize then was that this moment would be a weight I'd carry with me for the rest of my life.

CHAPTER 19
DETERMINATION

As I found myself not too far from home, now driving through the rolling hills and twilight skies of New Jersey, a sense of familiarity washed over me. The stretch of highway I was on – a path I'd traveled countless times before – was lined with an array of hotels, most notably the recognizable Hilton and Best Western brands. As I glanced at the welcoming lights of these establishments, a thought crossed my mind: should I stop for the night? It was becoming increasingly clear that I had been on this journey for quite some time, navigating through the twists and turns of the state all on my own, with nothing but my thoughts to keep me company. I couldn't help but marvel at how I had managed to drive this distance by myself, feeling both exhausted and somewhat accomplished at the same time – a sense of pride that I hadn't expected to feel.

The road had been long – seemingly endless – and I had turned to prayer more times than I could count, seeking strength and guidance to push through the darkness that had been lingering over me like a cloud. The evidence of my emotional journey was evident, as my face was likely stained by tears, a silent testament to the struggles I had faced along the way – struggles that I couldn't yet bring myself to talk about. The bright lights of the hotels flickered in the distance, their names glowing against the backdrop of the night like beacons calling out to weary travelers. As I gazed out at the scenery, I couldn't help but think about the convenience of using my credit card to book a room – the simplicity of it all was tempting. It would be so easy to stop, to give in to the fatigue that was creeping in, but something held me back – a spark within me that refused to be extinguished.

Deep down, I felt a strong urge to press on – a sense of determination that I couldn't ignore. I had come this far, and the thought of giving in now didn't sit right with me – it felt like surrendering to the darkness that had been following me for so long. So, I steered the car ahead, determined to continue my journey through the night, chasing the goal that awaited me just a little further down the road – a goal that seemed to be shrouded in uncertainty yet felt strangely attainable. As the miles flew by, I found myself wondering – maybe that's what dealing with grief has to look like: the determination to go forward, no matter how daunting the journey may seem – the courage to keep moving, even when all you want to do is stop.

CHAPTER 20
WAVES OF EMOTION

As I finally rounded the bend and pulled into my driveway, I could hardly wrap my head around the fact that I had made the journey home in under ten hours – a feat that seemed almost impossible. For as long as I could remember, this particular trip had always taken me around thirteen hours, especially with the unpredictable traffic that usually accompanied it, like a tiresome companion I had grown accustomed to. It was almost surreal – the kind of thing you see in movies but rarely experience in real life. I pushed the door open, and the familiar creak of the hinge was like music to my ears.

I reflected on my journey – the one quick stop for gas, the brief stretch to get the blood flowing, and the long, winding roads that seemed to have flown by in a colorful blur. I couldn't shake the image that was etched in my mind – my car speeding along the winding roads, soaring over mountain incisions and peaks, almost like something straight out of an adrenaline-pumping chase scene from a blockbuster movie, the kind that leaves you on the edge of your seat and your heart in your mouth.

As soon as I parked my car and turned off the engine, a wave of mixed emotions—relief, joy, and exhaustion—washed over me. It felt like a perfect storm of emotions converging all at once. I opened the door, leaving my overnight bag in the rear seat, and took a moment to inhale the familiar scent of home that greeted me like a warm hug. The smell of fresh flowers, clean laundry, and the faint aroma of my favorite coffee beans came flooding back, filling me with a comforting sense of familiarity.

Just as I stepped toward the front door, my middle daughter, Krista, came rushing to meet me—her bright smile and sparkling eyes like a beacon of hope and joy. The moment she wrapped her arms around me, I felt the floodgates open. A sense of being home, with the people I loved, and in a place where I belonged overwhelmed me. No longer able to hold back, I collapsed into her embrace, letting the tears stream down my face while I sobbed—a mixture of relief, happiness, and a deep sense of accomplishment. It was an overwhelming tidal wave of emotion, and I couldn't quite believe that all of this was happening right now, in this moment, in this place.

Lou and his niece, Krista, at his post-wedding gathering in January 2017.

CHAPTER 21
SHATTERED

The day after my return home was a surreal experience – a blur of emotions I could hardly pin down. I found myself sitting in silence, holding my breath as I waited for that inevitable call that I knew would come yet dreaded all the same. It was early morning, and the world outside was waking up – the sun rising over the horizon, birds chirping their gentle melodies – but inside, I felt a heavy weight on my chest. The stillness was oppressive, and I couldn't shake off the feeling of being trapped in a nightmare from which I couldn't awaken. Eventually, I took the initiative and made a call to the hospice social worker, desperately seeking answers and reassurance. When she called me back, I was filled with apprehension and hope – a mix of emotions that left me restless and uncertain.

During our conversation, she spoke about the hospice program with an understanding and gentleness that eased some of my anxiety – her words were a soothing balm to my frazzled nerves. Her kind words about the quality of care provided were a welcome comfort amidst the turmoil – they reminded me that I wasn't alone in this journey and that there were people who cared and were willing to help. I clung to those words, letting their comfort wash over me like a warm breeze on a cold winter's day.

Meanwhile, my daughters moved around the house like they were walking on eggshells – their footsteps quiet, their voices hushed. They were obviously trying to gauge my emotional state, unsure of how to approach the situation. They didn't know how to navigate the complex web of emotions that I was feeling, and their uncertainty left me feeling protective of them – I didn't want them to get hurt. My youngest, in particular, was still grappling with denial – that inevitable defense mechanism that shields us from the pain of reality. It inevitably reminded me of the painful memories two years prior when I had lost a close friend. The memory of that loss was still raw, still tender – and it brought back all the emotions I thought I had buried. That kind of emotional distance can be both protective and isolating, and I felt it deeply – like a gash that refuses to heal.

Later that day, I went for a walk with my neighbor – a woman who had become a steady source of support during this time. She was a presence that soothed my frazzled nerves, a reminder that I didn't have to face this alone. She maintained a quiet presence, allowing me to express whatever was on my mind whenever I felt the need. She let me talk, letting me unravel the threads of my thoughts and emotions. At other moments, she walked in silence alongside me, respecting the complexities of my feelings.

During our walk, she handed me a reassuring card that contained a heartfelt message – her words were a reminder that we would navigate this journey together, no matter how challenging it might be. The gesture was simple, but it was a powerful reminder of the strength of human connection.

In the following hours, as I slowly came to terms with the reality of my situation, two friends invited me out for snacks and drinks at a local waterside restaurant. The atmosphere was light, with the warm sun shining down on us — but I couldn't help but express my concerns about how my daughters were short on family support, specifically aunts and uncles. The weight of their uncertainty was like an added burden on my shoulders, a reminder that I wasn't just fighting for my own sanity but also for theirs.

I looked at my friends and pointedly told them that they needed to step up and fill that role. I needed them to be the support system my daughters required — to be the ones who could offer a shoulder to cry on, a listening ear, and a comforting presence. Their responses were immediate and warm; they both exchanged glances and said in unison, "Duh, what do you think we have been doing?"

The lightheartedness was a balm to my worried heart — a reminder that I wasn't alone in this journey and that I had a community willing to rally around my family during this difficult time.

CHAPTER 22
THE PRICE OF LOVE

As fate would have it, I received the devastating phone call that shattered my world – he had passed away. His wife was not home at the time and was in a location where she had no cell signal to receive the news, leaving her temporarily unreachable. The individuals delivering this heartbreaking message reached out to me first, urgently asking for an alternate contact number because they were unable to get through to her. When they called me back after failing to reach her, I was overwhelmed with disbelief and sorrow, and that is when I let out a blood-curdling scream – a primal response that echoed in the space around me. The anguish was palpable, and I felt as though I was frozen in that moment, unable to process the reality of the situation. I cannot say for sure if anyone present had ever witnessed such a reaction from me before; raw, unfiltered emotion spilled out in the form of that anguished cry, leaving me and those around me stunned.

It felt as though my heart had splintered into a million irreparable pieces – the intensity of the pain coursed through me, leaving me breathless and overwhelmed. The tears flowed incessantly, a relentless stream that seemed as if it would never cease. In the midst of that chaos, my mind struggled to come to terms with the loss, desperately seeking a way to cope with the anguish that threatened to engulf me. Amid my sorrow, my daughter instinctively ran out to fetch our next-door neighbor, a dear friend who had always been a source of support in times of distress. As I sat on the floor, surrounded by the warmth and love of my family and friends, the weight of the loss felt suffocating, almost unbearable – the atmosphere was heavy with grief. I felt like I was drowning in a sea of despair. My husband held me close, providing a steady presence as I wept uncontrollably. At the same time, my daughter and best friend enveloped me in their embrace. The moment was raw and sacred – an experience marked by profound sadness yet also marked by the undeniable understanding of our shared grief.

In this moment filled with intense emotion and heartache, my daughter and I found a flicker of solace as we recited the Lord's Prayer together – the familiar cadence of the words, deeply ingrained in our hearts, offered a semblance of peace and comfort amidst the devastation that surrounded us. Each phrase felt like a lifeline, grounding us in a reality that seemed utterly shattered – the words provided a sense of stability in a world that had been turned upside down. As we uttered those sacred words, I could feel the bond between us strengthening, as if we were standing together against the tide of grief washing over us – the prayer became a source of unity, a way for us to find comfort in each other's presence. The memory of that scene – the two of us, lost in prayer, cocooned in the love of those around us – plays over and over in my mind. It serves as a poignant reminder of the intimate connection we shared, one that is now tinged with the acute pain of his absence – a pain that I will carry with me for the rest of my life.

In my reflections on that heart-wrenching moment, I find some degree of consolation in the promises of hope offered by Christian scriptures – the passage from the book of Revelation resonates deeply within me, articulating a future devoid of death, a place where tears will no longer exist, and a new

Jerusalem will rise. This profound message of eternal peace provides a sense of reassurance, a glimmer of hope that one day, we will be reunited with our loved ones in a realm untainted by suffering or sorrow – the thought of such a promised future offers me strength as I navigate the challenging journey of grief, reminding me that love transcends even the deepest of losses. As I hold onto this hope, I find the courage to move forward, one step at a time, knowing that I am not alone in my grief – I am surrounded by the love and support of those who care for me. I am strengthened by the bond that I share with my daughters.

CHAPTER 23
THE COMMON BOND

Those moments – the ones that cut deepest and leave an indelible mark – become seared into our memory, etched into our consciousness in a way that time cannot erase. They linger, reminding us of both the overwhelming weight of loss and the crushing weight of grief. It's crucial to recognize that while these moments are significant, they represent only a fragment of the broader narrative of life. This narrative – complex and multifaceted as it is – cannot be reduced to a single event or experience. We must keep in mind that such experiences, however profound and life-altering they may be, do not encompass the entirety of our existence or the stories we hold dear.

A few days later, I found myself behind the wheel once more, making the long – and arduous – journey back with my three daughters in tow, bound for the funeral. The drive was once again filled with a sense of heaviness, a palpable reminder of the somber occasion that lay ahead. Yet, within the confines of the vehicle, the atmosphere was punctuated – and sometimes even lifted – by the innocent chatter of my girls, who were in the backseat sharing stories, laughter, and occasionally bickering with one another. Their lighthearted conversations – a welcome respite from the weight of our grief – provided a stark contrast to the reason for our trip, a small glimmer of normalcy amid the emotional turmoil we were carrying. As I glanced in the rearview mirror, I couldn't help but notice how their carefree chatter seemed to bounce off the somber mood that had settled over us, creating a sense of poignant and profound tension.

As we traveled along the winding roads – the scenery blurring together as we navigated the twists and turns – my daughters expressed their curiosity and surprise regarding my decision to get a tattoo of his name at this stage in my life. They found it both intriguing – a bold expression of grief and love – and perhaps a bit unconventional, considering the age at which I was making such a permanent choice. Their reactions ranged from playful teasing to thoughtful contemplation as they tried to understand the significance of that act. It seemed like a bold statement in their eyes, and I could sense their admiration mixed with a hint of concern. This journey was more than just a drive; it was a moment of shared grief, familial bond, and a testament to the way in which we were all processing our loss together. As I watched them navigate their own emotions – oscillating between sadness and curiosity – I was reminded that even in the darkest moments, there is always the potential for growth, for healing, and for a deeper understanding of ourselves and those around us.

CHAPTER 24
REFLECTIONS AND A EULOGY

I knew it was important for Lou's wife that we pay our respects and see him lying in repose before he was cremated. That last image I wasn't sure about at first – I hesitated, questioning whether it was something I truly wanted to do. Reflecting on it now, even after so many years have passed, I can still vividly recall how difficult that moment was. It was truly awful and horrific. I felt lost, unsure of how to comfort my three daughters while also trying to hold myself together. At that moment, my maternal instincts kicked in, and I found myself telling my girls to lock arms – a simple, instinctual gesture, but it felt necessary. We needed to physically support each other in that overwhelming moment. The sight before us was heartbreaking; Lou didn't resemble himself at all – the disease had taken its toll on his body, transforming the man we once knew. I often remind my clients that while the end of someone's story is a crucial part of the grieving process – our grief work, my grief work – it is just one chapter in their life. The end-of-life image can sometimes be the most vivid, but it's essential to remember that it doesn't define the entirety of their journey.

What I do for myself, and what I have suggested for my daughters, is to use a picture you are fond of as a screensaver—a tangible reminder of the person they once were at their best. This practice encourages us to remember so much more of that story prior to that horrible image. By holding onto cherished memories, we can work through our grief more effectively, acknowledging the fullness of the person we've lost. This approach allows us to celebrate their life, honor their memory, and navigate the complex emotions that accompany loss.

At the funeral service, I was honored to take the role of eulogist, a responsibility that weighed heavily on my heart but also felt like a tribute to a life that had meant so much to so many. As I stood before family and friends, gathered to pay their respects and share in the collective grief, I sought to encapsulate the essence of the person we had lost.

In my reflections, I felt a profound connection to the emotions surrounding this moment, and I found myself inspired by a particularly poignant line from Lady Gaga's song *"Joanne."* The words echoed in my mind: *"Every part of our aching hearts needs you more than the angels do."* This sentiment resonated deeply with me, capturing the raw, heartfelt longing we all felt in that space. It articulated the depth of our sorrow, illustrating how desperately we needed the presence of our loved one in our lives, even more than those who reside among the celestial beings—a painful acknowledgment that their passing has left an unifiable void.

This line not only reflected the pain of loss but also the enduring love we carry for someone who has passed, reminding us of the irreplaceable role they played in our lives.

Lou holding his god daughter Amanda in 1993.

CHAPTER 25
DOODLING GRIEF

My grief is like – a doodle, swirling around me, heavier and defined at times, and sometimes light, a spontaneous and unrefined expression of emotions that varies in intensity and form. Some days, it feels almost surreal to confront the reality that he is no longer here with me; it is as if I am caught in a trance, unable to comprehend the permanence of your absence. On those days, I often find myself paralyzed by indecision, struggling to determine the course of my actions or even my thoughts. The urge to reach for my cell phone and call him arises instinctively – an automatic reflex that collides painfully with the jarring reminder that you will not answer. The haunting realization sweeps over me: the voice I once knew so well is now silenced. I no longer possess a recording of his voice, a memory I assumed would remain intact. It's a harsh truth I'm still grappling with – it hasn't been easy to come to terms with.

Other times, there are days when the sharp pain of your departure recedes into the background, no longer dominating my thoughts. On those days, I muster a tentative hope that I will navigate through this labyrinth of grief, one step at a time, one day at a time. It dawned on me the other day that perhaps grief resembles the act of sketching – when you open up a blank page, you are greeted by a world of possibilities. Each stroke of the pencil, each thought, and memory can lead to unexpected and varied outcomes. Some moments bring forth clarity and comfort, while others plunge me into depths of sorrow and confusion that are hard to articulate. In those moments, I'm reminded that grief is a mysterious and intricate process that requires patience and understanding.

Reflecting further on this analogy, I realize that some lines in my doodle are stronger and more pronounced while others are lighter and less defined. The heavier lines reflect the moments of profound grief, the days when the weight of my sadness is overwhelming. In contrast, the softer, lighter lines represent the fleeting instances of joy or acceptance that occasionally break through the heaviness. This interplay of heavy and light lines captures the essence of my grief, which is multifaceted and ever-shifting. Just like a doodle that evolves with each new stroke, my grief continues to transform and reshape itself as I journey through life without you. There are moments when I feel lost in this ever-changing landscape, unsure of what the future holds – but I'm trying to be patient, to trust the process, and to allow myself to heal. My grief is like a doodle, a complex tapestry of emotions that defies any simple explanation – and it's a reminder that I'm still navigating the twists and turns of this uncharted territory.

CHAPTER 26
JUST BROKEN

About two months after he died – a loss that still felt like an open wound – I embarked on a September trip to Vermont, driven by a desire to find solace in the midst of turmoil. I decided to visit a monastery, seeking a sense of peace that had eluded me since his passing. The tranquil atmosphere of the monastery was a balm to my aching heart, but it was during one of my solitary walks, wandering through the picturesque streets, that I stumbled upon a charming shop. The store was adorned with Christmas ornaments, and lively holiday music filled the air, creating a festive atmosphere that seemed to belie my somber mood.

As I wandered through the shop, I couldn't help but feel a deep sense of sorrow and longing. Each ornament seemed to hold a different memory, a different story, but none resonated with me as profoundly as the delicate amber bottle of bootleg whiskey that caught my eye. Memories of you flooded my mind – memories of the exceptional whiskey you had gifted me from your trip to Kentucky the year before. I vividly recalled that Christmas morning when I had shared the whiskey with my dearest friend, cherishing the moment together. The sight of the ornament brought tears to my eyes, and I was unable to contain my grief.

The kindness of a stranger

The shop owner, noticing my distress, approached me with a gentle smile. Her kind eyes and compassionate demeanor put me at ease, and I found myself pouring out my heart to her, whispering, "I just lost my brother." I never caught her name, but her response was a poignant reminder of the power of human compassion. She looked at me with a profound understanding, offered her condolences, and retreated to retrieve a box of tissues. With her simple act of kindness, I felt a glimmer of peace that I thought had been lost forever.

I gathered my strength, took the little bottle from the tree, and purchased it. As I expressed my gratitude to the shop owner, I felt a sense of peace wash over me. The darkness that had enveloped me since his passing seemed to recede, replaced by a sense of hope and renewal. Driving through the familiar winding roads of the mountains, I couldn't help but feel grateful for the keepsake that now sat beside me, a tangible reminder of the kindness that had helped me navigate the darkest of times.

The power of kindness

Her name may have remained a mystery, but the impact of her kindness was undeniable. The small act of offering me tissues and a comforting word was a ray of light in my moment of darkness. As I hung the keepsake on a branched tree at home, I couldn't help but reflect on the compassion I had encountered that day. The Christmas gift of empathy that she had given me was a testament to the fact that even in the depths of grief, kindness has the power to uplift and heal. The little bottle of bootleg whiskey now serves as a reminder of the transformative power of kindness, a symbol of the enduring legacy of compassion and empathy that my brother's memory embodies.

CHAPTER 27
STILL TALKING

Conversations Beyond Time

I continue to have conversations with him - often imagined, sometimes aloud - although the responses remain forever silent. The quietness is a heavy reminder of his absence. If only he could respond. What a universal yearning - a common theme that echoes through countless songs, verses, and stories.

Despite sending letters, making calls, and writing messages that went unanswered, I find myself searching for alternative means to bridge the silence. I find solace in revising lyrics to songs such as "I'll Be Missing You" by Puff Daddy and "Empty Garden" by Elton John. These revisions allow me to process my emotions and pay tribute to the memories I shared with him. I share these revised lyrics with my daughters and his nieces - the next generation - in the hope that they will find comfort in the words, just as I do.

I often share these revised songs with people who don't know him, and when they read my words, they begin to understand the depth of my grief. They get a glimpse of the void left by his departure. It forever changed me, but the writing helps – it helps me find meaning, find solace, and slowly heal. Writing, writing prompts, and this therapeutic process help me come to terms with the harsh reality that you are no longer here and you will not return.

From the moment you disclosed your cancer diagnosis - that unforgettable day – I knew our time together was limited. I remember the weight of those words, the silence that followed, and the unspoken fears that lingered in my mind.

Journaling: A Therapeutic Outlet

A therapeutic technique to process grief is journaling— whether it's free-style, answering prompts, or simply writing out your feelings so they get out of your head. The act of writing them down makes the emotions concrete and tangible, giving substance to your thoughts. It's a way to unburden your heart and mind.

I wish I had journaled more about his loss—capturing the ebb and flow of emotions—but the process of writing this now has been liberating. I know that he would be floored by the depth of my feelings; I don't think he had a clue how his loss would have impacted me. It's a painful realization but also a testament to the bond we shared.

CHAPTER 28
STORYTELLING CAN HEAL

We had different tastes in music, but there was an occasional crossover now and then, a blending of genres, and a shared appreciation for specific artists. I vividly remember his schoolboy crushes—vivid, all-consuming, and full of unspoken dreams. One of these early infatuations was for Stevie Nicks, the enchanting voice and ethereal presence of Fleetwood Mac—a fascination that I would lovingly tease him about in later years. I would often smile and say, "Oh, I forgot, you were in love with Stevie Nole... the Queen of Rock 'n' Roll." Little did I know that this was only one of many early crushes, one that would be joined by another equally captivating artist—Melanie, of *Brand New Key* fame.

Melanie, with her striking long dark hair—attractively parted in the middle—became an instant object of fascination for him, the epitome of the iconic '60s. He would practically drool when looking at an album cover, each image encapsulating an undeniable allure and charisma, to the point where it was almost impossible for him to tear his eyes away. When I heard the news of her recent passing, it stirred in me a minor yet unexpectedly significant emotional response. The news story seemed to reverberate in my mind, carrying me back to a different time and place. As I saw her name on the news, I was instantly transported back to my own past—a vivid flashback to the many afternoons I spent with him in my

70

room, listening to her mesmerizing *Live at Carnegie Hall* album — an experience that evoked a flood of memories.

I was initially tempted to spiral into the depths of those recollections. However, I decided to channel this moment into an opportunity for storytelling - passing on a piece of our shared past to my daughters. I swiftly gathered the fragments of this bygone era and sent the news story, along with pictures of Melanie and the Live at Carnegie Hall album, to my daughters. The exercise allowed me to share with them a relatable story about a young teenage boy navigating the intricacies of a first crush. As I watched them respond with a mixture of amusement and curiosity, we all smiled, our hearts filled with the nostalgia of that moment - a brief respite from the passage of time. For me, this was more than just a casual reminiscence - it was a testament to the power of shared memories, an opportunity to keep his memory alive through these small yet significant anecdotes.

I find it essential to pass these stories on to my daughters, reminding them of his formative years when the world was extensive and life seemed to stretch into eternity. It connects them to the person he was, beyond the impressions they have of him now - giving them a glimpse into the earlier moments that make up the tapestry of his story. By sharing these reminiscences, I am holding on to a piece of our past, even as the world around us continues to change.

CHAPTER 29
HIS POWERFUL LESSONS

Gratitude is an extraordinary gift that profoundly influences our lives – its remarkable ability to alter brain chemistry contributes to a sense of inner peace, emotional stability, and overall happiness. Numerous studies in psychology have highlighted the significant role that gratitude plays in mitigating feelings of anxiety, depression, and grief, which are challenges that many individuals encounter throughout their lives. Through my experiences, particularly during the brief but impactful months surrounding Lou's diagnosis and subsequent passing, I learned firsthand the transformative power of gratitude.

Despite receiving a devastating diagnosis that would ultimately lead to his demise, Lou demonstrated a remarkable capacity for gratitude. His approach to life during this period was inspiring – actively seeking opportunities to express appreciation and share positivity with others. Regularly, he would post uplifting memes and encouraging messages on social media platforms like Facebook, reaching out to friends and family, including myself and my daughters. His efforts did not go unnoticed; I found myself printing these sentiments and preserving them as cherished reminders of his resilient spirit. On the very same day he received the life-altering news about his health, Lou made a thoughtful gesture by sending flowers to his wife, demonstrating that even in the darkest moments, the light of gratitude can shine brightly.

Lou's unwavering attitude in the face of such adversity served as a powerful lesson in the importance of maintaining a grateful heart, regardless of life's challenges. His examples left me in awe, provoking deep reflections about my own capacity for strength and grace under similar circumstances. Lou's life became a poignant reminder that gratitude is a fleeting feeling and a deliberate practice that can sustain us through even the most difficult times.

Since Lou's passing, I have navigated the seasons marked by heartbreak and loss, and within that journey, I have found comfort in cherishing the many gifts his presence brought into my life. He was not just a friend; he was my rock and my confidant, someone with whom I could share my thoughts and feelings, especially during the era when landlines connected us. I often reminisce about our late-night discussions that spanned across states, with Lou in the Midwest and me on the East Coast. Despite the challenges posed by weather events like blizzards or hurricanes, we were always there for each other. One particularly vivid memory stands out, showcasing Lou's unwavering support and creativity. He came to the rescue during a challenging moment for my youngest daughter, who was struggling with a school project involving sugar cubes – he initially looked at me and told me to throw it out; the look on my face indicated to him that it wasn't going to happen. Lou took it upon himself to transform her vision into reality, crafting a detailed Central American pyramid. It's one of my favorite memories of him, as it is my daughter's.

As I reflect on these countless memories, I recognize that the list of reasons I am grateful for Lou's presence is endless. This practice of gratitude serves as a means to honor his memory while also providing me with the resilience needed to continue moving forward in life. By continually acknowledging the blessings he brought into my world, I am filled with determination to carry on his legacy of positivity and appreciation, finding strength in the lessons he left.

The transformative power of gratitude has become integral to my life's journey. As I continue to navigate the complexities of life, I am reminded that gratitude is not just a reaction to a specific event but a deliberate choice that requires effort and dedication. By making this choice, I can find solace in the memories of Lou's presence and move forward with a renewed sense of purpose. The ripple effect of his legacy continues to inspire me to cultivate a grateful heart, even in the face of adversity, and to share this gift with those around me.

CHAPTER 30
SO MANY WHAT IF'S

Grief is an overwhelming experience, much like carrying a heavy backpack filled with stones that seem to multiply as time goes on – each stone weighing us down with the weight of memories, promises unfulfilled, and the relentless questioning of what could have been. Recently, I had a conversation with someone about the burdens that grief imposes on us, and it struck me how we often find ourselves weighed down by an array of thoughts and feelings that linger long after our loved ones are gone, like a shadow that follows us, constantly reminding us of our loss. We grapple with countless "what ifs" and "I should haves" that loop in our minds, making it difficult to find any sense of peace – a fleeting feeling that seems to vanish into thin air.

Take, for instance, the nagging thought of what might have happened if he had decided to stop smoking when he was younger – a decision that could have potentially altered the course of events. It's a question that gnaws at the edges of my mind, a small stone in that already heavy backpack that seems to be getting heavier by the day. What if we had followed through on our whimsical idea of decorating his lawn with a quirky collection of 44 gnomes, a project I had once excitedly discussed with my girls but never executed? Those little moments feel so significant now, tugging at my heart with every memory of laughter and missed opportunities – a bittersweet reminder of the memories we shared. What if I had made one more phone call, a simple act that could potentially have changed something? Everything?

Reflections on a Complex Relationship

And then there's the haunting thought of not being able to face the truth of his illness. I should have been more honest and acknowledged the severity of the situation, but instead, I turned away – a decision that continues to haunt me to this day. He had the courage to confront it head-on, to share that burden with me, but I couldn't do the same – a decision that filled me with regret and self-doubt. Reflecting on our relationship brings a mix of emotions – a rollercoaster ride of feelings that I'm still trying to navigate. In all the years we spent together, I can recall only one actual confrontation we had, a singular disagreement in 2012 that arose when he canceled at the last minute for Thanksgiving dinner. – a moment that still feels like a raw wound, even after all these years.

Just minutes before we were set to eat, my phone rang – it was him, canceling our plans. I was furious – a feeling that I couldn't shake off, no matter how hard I tried. This led to a cascade of annoyance on both sides, creating a palpable tension that lingered for a while. The specifics of that incident have faded into the background over time, yet it was clear he was navigating a turbulent breakup at that moment, which added layers of complexity to our interaction – a complicated mix of emotions that we both struggled to process. Sibling squabbles are a natural part of life, I often remind myself, but in that instance, I believed it was something we would eventually look back on as a minor bump in the road during our holiday gatherings in our eighties – a nostalgic look back on a moment that, at the time, felt like the end of the world.

Reconciling Memories and Emotions

When I counsel clients, I often emphasize that such conflicts are an ordinary aspect of life, and it's vital to remember the way we reconciled afterward – a process that was both effortless and exhausting at the same time. Yet, despite my efforts to move forward, that moment still resurfaces in my thoughts, much like a pitcher who throws an immaculate game only to allow a hit in the final moments, disrupting what felt like an unstoppable flow – a feeling that I'm still trying to recapture, even now. I recognize that my recollection may romanticize our shared experiences, painting a picture that might not fully represent the reality of our lives – a bittersweet reminder that our emotions often taint our memories. However, I cling fiercely to the underlying message in all of this – the knowledge that he was always there for me, and beneath the weight of grief lies a powerful truth: I was loved deeply – a feeling that I'll continue to cherish, even in the darkest of times.

Lou is sitting with his niece Sara at a family event in 2006.

CHAPTER 31
LOOKING FOR SIGNS

There are an overwhelming number of books dedicated to the topic of signs from the afterlife—a concept that resonates deeply with me, often evoking feelings of comfort and curiosity. In my professional experience, I have encountered numerous clients who share their profound experiences involving signs from departed loved ones, each one unique and awe-inspiring in its own way. These signs can manifest in various forms, such as discovering an unexpected dime, finding a feather in an unusual place, or experiencing a vivid dream that feels more like a message than mere imagination. For some, the presence of specific numbers, music, or fragrances can evoke strong connections to their loved ones who have passed on.

A crucial point often overlooked is the open mindset required to acknowledge and understand these signs. I hold a firm belief in the existence of an afterlife and the presence of a higher power, which makes these accounts all the more significant in not just understanding their connection but also appreciating the deep emotional solace they provide.

The day following my retirement marked a profound transition—a palpable shift in identity that I continue to grapple with and redefine. I woke up early, instinctively feeling as though my body was still in work mode, ready to engage with the tasks of the day and carry on with the momentum of my pre-retired self. Since I was already awake, I decided to head to the kitchen to prepare my morning coffee, embracing the quiet calm that the morning hours had to offer and momentarily pushing aside thoughts of retirement and the uncertainty that came with it. As I inserted the coffee pod into the machine, my gaze wandered out the window, where my unkempt yard lay before me, with scattered leaves, fallen branches, and blanketed with the residual silence of the night. To my surprise, perched on a branch of a tree, I spotted an incredibly vibrant red cardinal. The bird appeared to be looking directly at me from a distance, perched with an air of serenity and exuding a silent understanding that resonated with me on an inexplicable level. Our eyes locked for a moment, the world around us fading into the background as time lost its grip on reality. At the same time, the roomy space allowed our connection to grow more profound and mysterious.

I recall that the world seemed to stand still as we shared that connection; I felt suspended in a parallel universe where memories of the past, memories of the present, and expectations from the future coexisted. I cannot recall how long we shared that connection, but it felt meaningful — almost like a milestone in my transition, granting me the courage to leap from one identity into another. The spell was temporarily broken as I took in the fragrance of coffee wafting through the air, making my coffee look alluring. However, before I could re-establish contact with my daily routine, the cardinal suddenly took flight — a delicate rustling of its wings, dissolving the stillness and taking that serenity with it. The cardinal's departure left me in a trance, momentarily forgetting about the rich aroma of coffee wafting through the air, wondering if I had truly experienced this moment, looking for some connection that allowed me to transcend the ordinary. In that fleeting moment, there was no doubt in my mind that this was a sign from Lou — a message of reassurance. It was an encounter that transcended explanation; sometimes, you know. It felt as if Lou was communicating with me, saying, "Hey, sis, you've done well. I'm here for you, guiding you every step of the way." That moment encapsulated everything I believed, reinforcing the significance of our connection even in his absence.

CHAPTER 32
TURNING TO A HIGHER POWER

I continue to find solace and comfort in my higher power, thoroughly convinced that the maker of the universe — the sky, and the earth, and the rivers, and all that lives here — was able to handle my anger, and in doing so, helps me navigate the darkest recesses of my soul.

I sometimes return to my Catholic roots and the symbolism rooted in the different traditions, those time-honored pearls of wisdom passed down through generations, traditions that have helped shape my understanding of the world and my place within it. Sometimes, I look to the traditions found in Holy Week and Easter, times of profound introspection and self-discovery.

The Easter candle carries profound significance in my life and spiritual journey — a symbol of hope, redemption, and the promise of new life. This remarkable candle is lit only thrice throughout the church year, filling each occasion with deep meaning, reflection, and introspection. The times it is ignited — during the Easter season to celebrate the resurrection of Christ, at baptisms to symbolize the initiation into the Christian faith, and during funerals to honor the passage from this life into the next — serve as poignant reminders of hope renewal and the enduring light that Christ brings into our lives, guiding us even in our darkest hours.

When I attend Easter vigils and witness the lighting of this candle, it evokes a powerful sense of hope. It signifies the radiant light that emerges from the resurrection of Christ—a beacon of light that illuminates the path ahead and reassures me of the promise of new life. Each flicker of the flame encourages a faith that supports and uplifts us during our darkest moments when the world seems to have lost its way. The Easter candle stands as a shining light, illuminating our path and inspiring us to embrace the renewal that comes with Christ's resurrection—a time of transformation, healing, and growth.

The Christian scriptures offer a wealth of hope that resonates deeply within me—a sense of hope that I cling to when the world around me seems to be falling apart. A specific passage from the Book of Revelation comes to mind, one that I had the honor of having read at my mother's funeral: "There will be no more death or mourning or crying or pain, for the old order of things has passed away." Each time I hear these words recited, memories of my mother flood my mind, and I am reminded of the sacrifices she made, the love she shared, and the lessons she taught me; I am also reminded of Lou, who also holds a cherished place in my heart—a testament to the enduring power of love and the human spirit.

Every Easter vigil becomes more than just a religious observance; it transforms into a profound moment of connection with my past, a time to reflect on the journey that has brought me to this point, and a reminder of the love shared with those who have departed. The significance of the Easter candle resonates powerfully, underscoring its presence in our lives during critical moments—moments of transition, of growth, and of transformation. As it is lit—whether to celebrate the joyous resurrection of Christ, to welcome a new member into the faith through baptism, or to honor a loved one's passing—its light represents the embodiment of Christ, leading us toward new life and instilling a sense of renewal and hope, even in the face of loss, and uncertainty.

There are passages in all the great traditions that speak to grief, loss, and solace—a testament to the shared human experience and the power of faith to heal and transform. If you are so inclined, let them comfort you; let them heal you; let their words soak into your soul and guide you on your own journey of self-discovery and growth.

Anita and Lou were at a backyard barbecue in the summer of 1963.

CHAPTER 33
A GESTURE OF LOVE

I have never considered myself to be someone who is particularly enthusiastic about tattoos – while they have never really piqued my interest, I have always maintained a neutral stance toward them. I don't personally desire to have one, but I am completely fine with others choosing to get tattoos, including my daughters. In fact, their decision to adorn their bodies with ink doesn't bother me in the least. There was a fleeting moment in my life, shortly after the events of September 11, 2001, when I did contemplate getting a tattoo myself – the notion crossed my mind that I might want to ink a flag or some symbol of patriotism to show my support for the country in that uncertain time. However, that impulse quickly faded as I began to weigh the potential pain associated with the tattooing process – the thought of enduring that kind of discomfort was daunting. Ultimately, I dismissed the idea rather swiftly.

Lou, on the other hand, had several tattoos. Although I couldn't quite recall the specific designs or meanings behind them, I did remember that he had expressed interest in adding a few more to his collection in the future – an enthusiasm that I had observed without much interest. As we found ourselves driving to Cincinnati for the funeral – a somber occasion that prompted a multitude of emotions – I felt a shift in my perspective. The emotional toll of the journey and the gravity of the situation prompted me to reconsider my previous attitude toward tattoos; I began to see them in a different light. During that painful, hours-long drive – filled with reflections, memories, and some poignant laughter – I decided to get a tattoo. I envisioned a design that would be discreet yet meaningful; I imagined a tattoo on my ankle, allowing me the option to lift my pant leg to reveal it whenever I wanted to share what it symbolized with others.

In that moment, I understood – in a way that I hadn't fully grasped before – what we do for love and how the smallest gesture can hold the deepest significance. A few months later, I found myself getting a tattoo of a heart with his name inscribed on it – a simple yet powerful symbol – placed discreetly on my ankle. It would be my first and last tattoo, a lasting tribute that I could always carry with me.

CHAPTER 34
TOYS AND MEMORIES

Moments of nostalgia can play a significant role in helping us cope with loss – that bittersweet feeling that tugs at our heartstrings and nudges cherished memories to the forefront of our minds. For me, this is especially true – and perhaps even more pronounced – with a couple of muscle car ornaments I keep prominently displayed on my desk. I've got two of these miniature replicas, and one of them even finds its place on my Christmas tree each year, hanging proudly amidst the twinkling lights and vibrant decorations. This particular ornament holds a special significance, a sentimental value that goes beyond its mere aesthetic appeal because it reminds me of him – a constant and comforting presence in my life.

He had a deep love for cars that started in his childhood when he would spend countless hours playing with Matchbox cars and Hot Wheels, his imagination running wild with the thrill of racing and speed. The thrill of car chase movies was something he truly enjoyed, and he had dreams of restoring a muscle car one day, which added to his passion for automobiles – a passion that only seemed to grow stronger with time. The muscle car ornaments serve as a poignant reminder of his enthusiasm and dedication to this hobby, a treasured memory that I cherish deeply.

In addition to the muscle car ornaments, there's another set of decorations on my tree that evoke fond memories: the Minion ornaments – those adorable yet quirky little yellow figures that never fail to bring a smile to my face. These ornaments remind me and my daughters of him, even though he was not a fan of the Minions at all. In fact, he had such a strong dislike for them that he would often make us laugh until we cried with his colorful descriptions of those "ugly yellow pill people," his words dripping with disdain yet delivered with such humor and wit. His exaggerated tales were always a source of laughter, and his distaste for the Minions became a running joke in our family – a lighthearted, humorous anecdote that still brings us joy to this day.

After he passed away, I stumbled upon some Minion ornaments, and I felt an inexplicable urge to get them – as if it was a sign, a way to keep his memory alive. It seemed only fitting to hang them on the tree as a way to remember him, to honor his spirit and his love for humor. During the holiday season, we would gather around the tree, reminiscing about him while sharing laughs over how he used to make fun of those little characters. Over time, the Minions have grown to become a symbol of our connection to him, a delightful mix of memories that elicit both laughter and a sense of loss at the same time – a bittersweet reminder of what we've lost, yet a celebration of the joy he brought to our lives.

Interestingly, I've found that these Minions have turned into a quirky little tradition in my life – a way to keep his memory close to my heart. Friends know about my fondness for the Minion jokes, and they often send me memes that keep the laughter going, a reminder that even in the midst of grief, there is still room for humor and joy. As a surprise gift for my retirement, a friend even treated me to a Minion coloring book, which was just the icing on the cake – a thoughtful gesture that brought tears of joy to my eyes. Every time I pick it up, I can't help but chuckle, thinking about how much he would have laughed at this whole situation – the absurdity of it all, the humor in finding joy in something so seemingly silly. It's as if his spirit lives on through these decorations, reminding me to find joy and humor in every moment, even in the midst of reminiscing – to cherish the memories, yet to keep moving forward, embracing life with all its complexities and challenges.

CHAPTER 35
A CHRISTMAS CARD

He took the time that year – a rare luxury for someone so immersed in his lab work – to create a unique Christmas card that he sent out to friends, family, and colleagues. The card featured a stunning cross-section of some mineral, *perhaps a beautifully arranged specimen of quartz or amethyst*, that he had been examining under his microscope. Upon first glance, the intricate patterns and colors within the mineral's structure resembled a serene winter landscape – complete with trees dusted with snow – capturing the essence of the holiday season in a refreshingly unexpected way. The artistry of the card resonated with many who received it – a testament to the intersection of art and science, both disciplines brought together by his passion for discovery – blending the beauty of nature with the scientific curiosity that inspired its creation.

As the card made its way to mailbox after mailbox, it seemed to evoke a sense of wonder in all who laid eyes on it. Ever since that memorable year, I have made it a tradition to include that particular image in my holiday cards each year – a small yet meaningful way to honor his legacy and keep his memory alive. It has become a cherished part of my seasonal greetings, serving as a reminder of the sometimes-overlooked intersection between science and the warmth of the holidays and as a testament to the creativity that can emerge from a place of inquiry and discovery.

CHAPTER 36
MY CONSTANT
COMPANION

Grief takes on the role of an ever-present companion that lingers in the background, subtly shaping your thoughts and emotions — an abyss of feelings that still seem to be in their formative stages. The loss I experienced is always with me, an omnipresent reminder of what once was - a bittersweet reminder that has, over time, become an integral part of my being. He and I were often apart; he spent his formative years in New Jersey, while I encountered him primarily during family gatherings and reunions that were infused with love and an abundance of shared stories - the time he would spend with us was a welcome respite from our daily routines. New Year's Eve, in particular, held a special place in our hearts - that was our holiday, where the warmth of shared meals and conversations would fill the space with a sense of togetherness. Those days, though few and far between, were filled with a sense of normalcy and connection, an unspoken understanding that seemed to transcend the physical distance between us; but now, even years later, in the quiet moments when the world seems to slow down, the absence resonates deeply - a hollow echo of what could never be again.

Now, grief is not just a fleeting feeling; it feels as though it has become an integral part of my day-to-day existence - a constant undercurrent that ebbs and flows with each passing day. Even in my professional life, it has wedged itself into the therapy sessions I conduct with my clients, subtly altering my approach – every conversation, every interaction, a reflection of the loss I have endured. As I guide others through their own struggles, I find that grief walks alongside me, serving as an uninvited sidekick that silently reminds me of my own vulnerabilities. It is a constant reminder that while I strive to support others, I too carry the weight of my own experiences – a weight that, though not crushing, is ever-present nonetheless. This coexistence creates a unique dynamic where grief is woven into the fabric of my reality, both shaping my understanding of human emotions and influencing my interactions with those around me.

CHAPTER 37
FINDING KEEPSAKES

I often find myself wondering how I can keep him close – how I can preserve the essence of our shared experiences in a way that feels tangible and enduring, like a warm, comforting embrace. One of the ways I connect with those memories is by frequently looking at the old photographs we took together – yellowed, dog-eared prints that have become treasured keepsakes over time. Though the images have faded over time and appear somewhat blurry, with visible creases and worn edges, they encapsulate moments that are rich with meaning and nostalgia – a nostalgia that is at once bittersweet and beautiful.

I have explored various photo editing programs, experimenting with their diverse range of features to breathe new life into these cherished memories. – features that can gently buff away dust and scratches or dramatically transform the visual landscape of an image. I have managed to colorize some of the pictures, transforming them from faded sepia tones into vibrant images that feel almost alive, imbued with a sense of color and vitality that seems to pulse with the life we once shared. For others, I have added decorative frames that enhance their presentation and give them a polished look – classic designs, muted colors, or simple textures that help bring out the intimacy, tenderness, and affection frozen in each frame. I've even taken the time to inscribe dates on some of the photographs, grounding the memories in specific moments that I can recall vividly – making them more than just faded images; instead, they become windows into our past, portals that allow me to revisit those days with clarity and warmth, like stepping into a dream I thought I'd forgotten.

One of our last meaningful exchanges revolved around his cherished rock 'em sock 'em robots – a conversation that felt both joyous and sad, a bittersweet swan song filled with the warm, rich timbre of shared experiences. It encapsulated a moment filled with elegance and poignancy. It reflected on our shared past and the simple pleasures that brought us so much joy – moments that transcended words, those small beauty-strewn vignettes of everyday life. In those conversations, I feel a connection that, while tinged with sadness, is also illuminated by the beauty of our shared history – an intricate tapestry of individual filaments and unbreakable threads, forming a larger whole that makes our past feel close, vivid, and undeniably ours.

Anita and Lou, in 1963 and in 2003

CHAPTER 38
MOVING ON WITH AND WITHOUT

I find myself – in quiet moments, and often when I least expect it – wishing he were here with me more than ever. There are moments, suspended in the ebb and flow of life when I feel an overwhelming sense of loneliness, a void that seems to grow larger with each passing day. Your advice has always been my guiding light, a beacon that has illuminated the path ahead and provided me with a sense of direction. Without it, I feel somewhat aimless – lost and drifting, without the comforting reassurance of your presence.

Last month, I celebrated my retirement – a significant milestone, a culmination of years of hard work and dedication – a moment that should have been filled with joy and excitement yet was tainted by your absence. However, the lack of your presence made the event bittersweet – an odd juxtaposition of happiness and sadness that I still grapple with.

My youngest spoke at the dinner, and Sara shared with me a written copy of her speech afterward, which included a brief paragraph where she mentioned Lou. It touched me deeply, knowing she wanted to honor his memory in that moment, acknowledging the impact he had on all of us. Yet, she chose not to read that part aloud, fearing it would bring tears to both our eyes – a heart-wrenching reflection of the profound emotions we still carry – the unspoken words and unseen tears that hold us together.

In her words, she assured me that he would be proud of the accomplishments I've made throughout my career – a validation that resonates deeply within me – reinforcing the connection we had and the memories we forged as a family. Those words meant a lot to me, an affirmation of the indelible mark Lou left on my life. These tender memories are the threads that weave our hearts together, the threads we hold onto as we navigate the uncertainties of life. It's perfectly acceptable to reflect on our loved ones – to meander through memories – and to seek signs or reminders of their presence in our daily lives. These thoughts bring me solace – a comforting reminder of the bond we share – a way to keep his spirit alive within me.

To commemorate my retirement, I created a unique dog tag featuring a cherished picture of us together – a token of remembrance, a tangible tribute to our enduring love. I wore it to the retirement dinner, a poignant reminder of the bond we shared – a bittersweet celebration of our past and a tentative step into the future. I often find myself pondering what Lou would say to me today if he were here – how his wisdom and encouragement would provide the clarity I need to navigate this new chapter in my life. In the silence, I imagine his words of reassurance – a soothing balm for my restless soul – guiding me through the trials and tribulations that lie ahead.

CHAPTER 39
STRENGTH OVER TIME

Grief is a profoundly exhausting and draining experience, one that can leave you feeling utterly depleted, as if every last bit of energy has been siphoned out of you. It's crucial to understand that this journey is not one to be underestimated - the emotional turmoil it brings can be overwhelming, and its weight can be crushing at times. There's a common phrase that floats around, often said to those dealing with loss: "It gets easier." But who exactly are these people making such claims - are they those who have experienced loss firsthand, or are they merely trying to offer a reassuring phrase in a time of need? It's a mystery, really. I find myself questioning their authority and the truth behind their words - what's their basis for saying this, and have they ever truly experienced the depths of grief?

In my role as a therapist, I have never really shared this sentiment openly with anyone. It's a thought that lingers in my mind, but when it comes to discussing it with friends or clients, I hold back - I don't want to give them false hope or mislead them into thinking that the pain will magically dissipate. I can't shake the feeling that I don't fully buy into that idea. So, let's set the record straight: I do believe that grief evolves over time - it's a dynamic, ever-changing process that can be difficult to navigate. It doesn't necessarily become easier; instead, it transforms into something different - a new, albeit unwelcome, normal. The sharp edges may soften, but the emotional weight remains, a constant reminder of what's been lost. Each day can bring new challenges, and you learn to navigate those changes in your own way - there's no one-size-fits-all approach to dealing with grief. What I do know for sure is that while the nature of grief shifts, the journey remains deeply personal and uniquely challenging - it's a solitary path that each person must walk alone.

Though the sharpness of my grief has softened as time has gone on—the edges have dulled, and the pain is no longer as all-consuming—certain days still carry the weight of loss. Birthdays, days that were once filled with laughter and celebration, anniversaries, and significant life events bring the missing piece of my heart to the forefront, causing a wave of sadness to wash over me, even after all this time. His loss has left an indelible mark on my journey, but so has the legacy of our relationship—a reminder of what we had and what could never be again. The memories we built together continue to shape who I am, and they hold deep meaning for me—a bittersweet reminder of what's been lost but also of what will always be.

Each recollection, whether joyful or bittersweet, carries a reminder of the connection we had—a connection that can never be severed—and the love that will always endure, a love that will forever be a part of me.

CHAPTER 40
FINDING RESILIENCE

One of the more thoughtful and personal suggestions I provide to my clients during special occasions - holidays, birthdays, or milestone events - is to consider making a donation to a charity in the name of the person they are honoring. This gesture not only celebrates the individual but also extends a helping hand to a meaningful cause that holds significance to them. While it is true that this act may go unnoticed by many, the impact of the gesture reaches far beyond the moment, touching the lives of those who benefit from the charity's work - often in profound and lasting ways. The name of the individual making the donation may only be seen by those responsible for entering the data - a necessary administrative task - but there is a much deeper connection formed when a donor chooses to support a cause that aligns with their values or passions.

Someone within the charity organization - perhaps a volunteer, staff member, or even the individuals directly benefiting from the donation - will acknowledge and appreciate this generous contribution, recognizing the individual who has chosen to support their mission and become a valued part of their community. In doing so, the donor becomes part of a larger community, one that shares their values and passions and contributes to efforts that resonate deeply. This fosters a sense of connection, purpose, and fulfillment. Ultimately, this practice of charitable giving in one's name serves to promote goodwill, create a positive ripple effect, and demonstrate that even small, seemingly insignificant actions can make a meaningful and lasting difference in the lives of others, inspiring a chain reaction of kindness and generosity.

CHAPTER 41
MUSIC HEALS

Music has always played a pivotal role in my journey through loss, offering solace and comfort during some of my darkest and most challenging moments. While I discovered many songs on my own, I also leaned on the vast resources of the internet—where endless recommendations are tailored specifically to help individuals process grief. In this soundscape exploration, I stumbled upon a handful of tracks that truly resonated with me, serving as emotional anchors throughout my healing process. I found myself playing these songs on repeat, fully immersing myself in their melodies and lyrics, which seemed to articulate the emotions I often struggled to express.

One of the standout tracks for me was *Dancing in the Sky* by Dani and Lizzy. This song encapsulates both the longing and hope that frequently accompany the grieving process. Another track that struck a deep chord was Elton John's *Empty Garden*, which poignantly touches on themes of loss and remembrance. Lady Gaga's *Joanne* provided comfort with its reflective and personal storytelling, while Ysaye Barnwell's *Wanting Memories* evoked a connection to cherished times now gone. I frequently turned to *Hear You Me* by Jimmy Eat World, a song that beautifully addresses remembrance and the enduring impact of those we've lost. Finally, Puff Daddy's *Missing You* resonated deeply, capturing the raw emotions of absence and

101

yearning in a way that felt achingly familiar.

Even today, years later, I still find myself listening to some of his favorite tracks. Whenever I hear one of those songs on the radio, I often remark to someone, "This was a song he loved." It's a small ritual I've held onto — keeping his memory alive in the melodies that shaped our shared moments.

Beyond music, certain films also became pillars of support throughout my grief journey. *"The Way"* stood out as a remarkable exploration of the transformative power of journeying through life, underscoring the unexpected connections we make with others who help us navigate our paths. Likewise, *"Ordinary People"* conveyed a moving narrative about the complexities of family dynamics and the resilience discovered through vulnerability. This film reinforced the idea that individuals often possess a strength they may not fully recognize until they face deep personal challenges. *"We Are Marshall"* also struck a chord with me, offering a portrayal of resilience in the wake of tragedy — reminding me of the strength that emerges from adversity and collective support.

Through music and film, I found a comforting embrace that helped me process my emotions, offering a means of understanding my grief and guiding me — bit by bit — toward healing. In these reflective moments, I was reminded of how Robert Kennedy found solace in reading poetry after the assassination of his brother, President John Kennedy. I, too, sought refuge in the writings of Rumi and the poetry of Mary Oliver. Their words resonated deeply, speaking to my inner thoughts and the complexities of human experience. Both offered me comfort and a profound sense of connection to something greater than myself.

In my search for solace, I not only turned to music and film but also found an invaluable outlet in reading and poetry. These mediums became my escape, providing space for personal reflection.

Somewhere in the many nooks and crannies of my home — tucked away in a forgotten corner — are several notebooks filled with poetry I wrote during my teenage years. These notebooks hold within them memories of my youthful creativity and emotional expression, capturing the essence of a time filled with intense exploration and feeling.

Among those pages, there are two or three poems that I collaborated on with Lou during my senior year of high school while he was beginning his sophomore year. I still have those poems somewhere. My kids have expressed interest in seeing them one day — perhaps someday, I'll share them.

I vividly remember the excitement we felt as we poured over the pages of James Michener's *"The Drifters,"* a novel chronicling the adventures of six young adults journeying through Spain. As we read and discussed the characters, we felt a deep connection to their stories, believing that we, too, were part of a larger, meaningful narrative. Our aspirations and dreams intertwined with those we found within the novel, marking us as young people eager to understand the world's complexities and our place within it.

Revisiting *"The Drifters"* now fills me with a sense of nostalgia. It's a tribute to our teenage years, which were filled with long, earnest conversations about everything — from the injustices we saw in the world to the dynamics of our families and the personal struggles we faced. Sometimes, it really did feel like it was just the two of us against the world.

Every now and then, we would indulge in sneaking a bottle of wine — using it as fuel for our deeper conversations about youthful crushes and the complicated emotions that accompanied them. Those were the moments where we truly felt alive—wrapped in the stories of our lives, unfolding page by page.

CHAPTER 42
MULTIPLE EMOTIONS

Grief counseling offers numerous advantages that can significantly aid individuals as they navigate through the complex emotions of loss. Although I was already familiar with the various theories associated with grief and emotional processing, I found myself struggling to apply this knowledge to my own experience. This personal realization led me to seek professional help by consulting a grief counselor—an action I had not initially anticipated taking. However, the experience proved immensely beneficial and transformative for me.

One of the most impactful insights I gained during these sessions was the understanding that it is entirely possible to experience multiple emotions simultaneously. *While I had intellectually grasped this concept beforehand,* hearing it articulated by a trained expert provided much-needed reassurance and validation. It was both surprising and liberating to learn that I could find moments of joy and laughter even while mourning a significant loss—and that doing so did not equate to dishonoring the memory of my loved one in any way. This shift in perspective allowed me to be more compassionate toward myself.

This particular sentiment resonates deeply with many clients seeking my support. They often express feelings of guilt or even betrayal when they catch themselves experiencing happiness or enjoyment in certain aspects of life after losing someone close to them. Many of them grapple with these feelings on a daily basis, as though finding joy is a violation of their grief. I frequently share an analogy that seems to help them navigate these conflicting emotions: consider a parent who feels upset or disappointed in their teenager's actions. Even in moments of frustration—or anger—the underlying love for that child remains constant, unshaken. This analogy serves as a gentle reminder that experiencing sadness or anger does not nullify the love and connection we hold for those we've lost.

It has been an immensely comforting thought for me personally, and I find it equally reassuring for those I work with. It helps them recognize that it's *okay* to embrace joy and welcome moments of laughter, even while they are still on their journey of grief. Acknowledging this duality can lead to a more nuanced and healing relationship with their emotions—a critical part of moving forward, not away from, the memory of their loved one.

CHAPTER 43
JOURNALING A JOURNEY

I kept a grief journal for quite some time, and it turned out to be incredibly significant during one of the most arduous periods of my life. Someone close to me had bought it as a gift, and I appreciated the gesture more than I initially realized. This particular journal was thoughtfully designed with various prompts, which made it much easier for me to express my feelings and reflections. For example, questions like *"What do you miss most?"* and *"What can you take with you?"* gave me a specific focus that I found immensely helpful as I navigated through my emotions. The prompt *"What do you cherish the most?"* was incredibly impactful—it made me pause, reflect deeply, and think about the good memories, which was comforting amidst the overwhelming sadness.

In addition to these thought-provoking questions, the journal also included adult coloring pages. Surprisingly, coloring became a wonderful way for me to find moments of distraction and relaxation amidst the emotional turmoil. Engaging in this creative activity allowed my mind to wander away from the heavier thoughts, giving me a much-needed mental break. The combination of reflective prompts and the meditative process of coloring created a unique approach to processing grief, one that resonated with me deeply during that challenging time.

Processing the anger that arises toward someone you once loved can be a complicated and emotional journey. When a loved one passes away, it's common for us to elevate their memory, almost casting them as saints in our minds. But the reality is, every person—no matter how much we loved them—had their flaws, their darker sides. They were not perfect, just as none of us are. We all carry a mix of light and shadow within us.

Personally, I often reflect on my own expressions of anger toward him, and I wonder how much I truly allowed myself to release those feelings. There are moments when I think back to his smoking habit, which troubled me deeply. I genuinely wished he had made the decision to quit. Sometimes, I still hear his voice in my head, and it ignites that familiar frustration. "Seriously, what were you thinking?" I want to shout at him, reminding him that he witnessed firsthand the devastating impact smoking had on my mother. It's a bitter pill to swallow, and I can't help but question why he didn't seem to care enough to change his ways.

Feeling anger in situations like this is not just common—it's natural. It's crucial to give yourself permission to feel that anger and not suppress it. One effective method to deal with those bottled-up emotions is to write them out—pour your raw thoughts into a letter, addressing every grievance, every hurt. Once the letter is complete, a powerful symbolic act can be to burn it, allowing those intense emotions to be released into the air, no longer confined to your mind. This ritual can bring a tangible sense of release, helping you process the complex layers of love, loss, and anger in a much healthier and more meaningful way.

CHAPTER 44
KEEP REMEMBERING, KEEP MOVING

Here I am now, faced with the necessity of moving forward. Like many who have experienced the sting of loss, I'm tasked with the challenge of finding a way beyond the sorrow. The road ahead is uncertain—fraught with emotional hurdles—but it's one that must be traveled.

Among the many lessons learned in this painful process is the realization that hope can still flourish, even in the aftermath of grief. I recall vividly a conversation I had with a close friend shortly after Lou passed away, where I expressed my belief that I would never be the same. In a sense, I suppose that assertion holds true; life as I knew it has undeniably changed—forever altered by the void that now exists. *Nevertheless*, there is also a subtle beauty in discovering how life continues to evolve despite that change.

Hanging on my wall is a piece of string art, a cherished creation made for me by a young boy who was once my close companion—my cousin. This art piece, crafted in his early teenage years, depicts a sailboat, its form both whimsical and nostalgic. Over time, some of the strands have become frayed, a testament to its age and the countless memories it holds. On the back of the artwork, he inscribed a heartfelt message— though the ink has faded, the meaning remains etched in my mind. With advancements in photo editing technology, I was able to capture an image of those sentimental words and restore them to a more transparent state, allowing me to revisit the emotions they convey whenever I need to.

He expressed to me, at the tender age of twelve, that my role in his life transcended that of just a cousin. I was, in his eyes, not only family but a dear friend. This statement—simple yet profoundly touching—has stayed with me throughout the years. I took a photograph of that message and decided to display it proudly alongside the string art itself, ensuring that the bond we shared was always visible and remembered.

This unique piece of string art, born from the imagination of a twelve-year-old boy, has evolved into a treasured family heirloom. It not only captures the innocence and creativity of youth but also symbolizes the enduring connections we forge in our lives. It serves as a reminder that moments of love and friendship can be found all around us—if we only take the time to seek them out and cherish them.

So, *seek out the treasures* you have and hold them close!

CHAPTER 45
A NEW PATH

I am still navigating this new path—sometimes feeling unsure, yet constantly pushing forward. Somehow, I find glimmers of hope in laughter, using my sense of humor as a vital tool to cope with the challenges that inevitably arise. Laughter doesn't just distract me from the challenging moments; it reminds me of my own strength.

Hope also thrives in my relationships, particularly with my adult children—whom I admit I often drive to the brink of frustration (and, yes, they do the same to me). Even amidst the chaos of these interactions, they serve as my steadfast support system, my rocks, and the unshakable foundation I lean on. Their laughter fills my heart with joy, and their playful teasing reminds me of the simple, uncomplicated pleasure of human connection. It's in these moments that I feel a sense of warmth, especially when they share how profoundly their uncle influenced their lives. The echoes of his impact resonate deeply within them, offering me a source of comfort that's both surprising and deeply appreciated.

Additionally, I remain endlessly grateful for the unwavering support of my friends, whose presence has been indispensable throughout this entire journey. Their companionship, like my children's, is a light in the dark. In my faith, I also find a renewed sense of hope—rooted in the promises of scripture that remind me there is a greater purpose at play, even in the moments when I feel most lost. Helping others has also become a cornerstone of my hope; I genuinely believe that in extending a hand to those in need, we end up lifting our own spirits as well.

Simple joys surround me in the world, from the cheerful chorus of birdsong in the mornings to the comforting companionship of my furry friends—my dog, my cats, and even my newest companion, a turtle. *Despite the shadows cast by loss,* joy is still out there, waiting to be uncovered. We just need to keep searching for it.

I've taken the time to document everything, not just as a tribute to my cousin, my brother, and my friend, but also to share a message of resilience and hope with others who may be navigating their own complex journeys through grief. Losing someone we love is an all-consuming and utterly exhausting experience—there's no easy way to go through it. It doesn't matter whether the loss is of a spouse, sibling, child, friend, or even a cherished pet; grief wears many faces, and each person's experience with it can be profoundly different. I've come across numerous memes that state, "Grief is the price we pay for love," and I can wholeheartedly say that this sentiment resonates with my own experience—deeply and without reservation.

In conversations with the people I work with, I often emphasize the revelations that come during our darkest moments. It's remarkable how many of us can uncover a well of inner strength that we never knew existed. This strength doesn't show itself until we truly need it—when there's no choice but to tap into it and push through the pain to begin healing. Moving forward after loss isn't about forgetting; it's about evolving and finding new ways to cope with the absence. We are often far more resilient than we give ourselves credit for.

Anita and Lou at his post-wedding gathering in January 2017.

This was the last picture ever taken together.

CHAPTER 46
AND SO I BEGIN

What else can I add about this challenging journey?

There are times when I talk to my daughters or close friends about my emotions, saying things like, "*I really miss him.*" In those moments, their responses are often, "*I know,*" which, while it may seem minimal, can provide a sense of comfort and validation. It's in these exchanges—these raw, vulnerable moments—that even a few words can foster a shared understanding, quietly acknowledging the weight of loss we both know exists but often struggle to articulate.

For those who find their grief overwhelming, it's vital to reach out for support. Whether through a structured support group, individual therapy sessions, or even grief coaching, these resources can offer significant help. It's important to remember that grief, though deeply personal, is not something you have to face alone. There are people and communities out there that can provide insight, share in your experience, and help you figure out how to cope with the sadness—step by step.

In addition to these formal avenues for support, countless other tools and resources can aid you on this journey. Writing prompts, for example, can help you put emotions that feel too heavy or complex into words to voice aloud. Music often serves as a powerful medium, evoking memories or emotions long buried. At the same time, films or even books can provide comfort and spark moments of reflection. They give us a safe space to confront what we are feeling. Additionally, creating personal traditions in memory of a loved one can foster a sense of connection and continuity. Lighting a candle on special dates, revisiting places you once shared, or simply keeping your favorite items close can create an ongoing relationship with the past.

While navigating grief is undoubtedly challenging—and at times utterly exhausting—so many different methods and resources can help ease the journey. The critical thing to remember is that while grief may never entirely disappear, it *does* evolve. It softens. And in that softening, there is space for hope, healing, and, eventually, peace.

I wish you peace.

"So, it's true—when all is said and done, grief is the price we pay for love."

CHAPTER 47
GRIEF CHARACTER

Unspoken Words

Write a heartfelt letter to the person you've lost, sharing everything you never had the chance to say. Don't worry about structure or grammar — let your emotions flow freely.

Memory Lane

Recall a vivid memory of the person who has passed away. Focus on sensory details — what you saw, heard, smelled, or felt — and explore how these memories continue to affect you.

The Empty Space

Visualize a physical space that represents your grief, whether it's a room, a landscape, or something symbolic. Describe this space in detail, capturing the emotions and sensations it brings to life.

The Things Left Behind

Write about an object or a place that has taken on new meaning because of its connection to the person you lost. Reflect on how it helps you remember them and its role in your grieving process.

Grief as a Character

Imagine your grief as a person or character in a story.

Describe how it looks, behaves, and interacts with you and the world around you.

The Conversation

Picture having a conversation with the person who has passed away. What would you say? How do you think they would respond? Use this imagined dialogue to express your feelings and thoughts.

The "What Ifs"

Reflect on a moment or event that you wish had turned out differently. Consider how things might have changed if the person were still here and how this "what if" shapes your grief.

The Empty House

Describe the first night in an empty house after the funeral. How does the silence feel? What memories linger in each room? Write about the overwhelming presence of absence.

A Love Letter Never Sent

Write a love letter to your spouse that you never had the chance to send. What would you have said if you knew it was your last chance to communicate with them?

The Rituals of Grief

Explore the small, daily rituals you continue to perform in honor of your spouse. Whether it's making their favorite cup of coffee, setting a place for them at the table, or visiting a special location—how do these rituals help or hinder your grieving process?

Unspoken Conversations

Imagine a conversation with your spouse's spirit or memory. What would you say to them now that they are gone?

What questions would you ask, and how might they respond?

The Weight of a Wedding Ring

Focus on the significance of your wedding ring after your spouse's death. What does it symbolize now? Reflect on the moment you decided to keep wearing it, take it off, or perhaps transform it into something new.

Packing Away a Life

Describe the experience of going through your spouse's belongings. Which items are the hardest to part with? What unexpected emotions arise as you sort through their things? How do you decide what to keep, give away, or discard?

The Last Words

Reflect on the last words exchanged between you and your spouse. Were they meaningful, mundane, or left unsaid? How do these final moments replay in your mind, and how do they shape your grieving process?

The Last Conversation

Write about the last conversation you had with your friend. What did you talk about? If you had known it was the last time you'd speak, what would you have said differently?

A Song That Reminds You

Think of a song that reminds you of your friend. Describe the memories or emotions that come up when you hear it. How does the song connect to your friendship and the loss you feel?

The Unfinished Plans

Reflect on the plans you and your friend made but never got to fulfill. Choose one particular plan or dream and imagine what it would have been like if you had the chance to experience it together.

A Place You Shared

Describe a place that holds special significance in your friendship, such as a café, park, or favorite hangout spot. How does this place feel now that your friend is gone? What memories does it bring to mind?

An Object Left Behind

Write about an object your friend left behind—a gift, a piece of clothing, or something they always carried with them. How does this object carry their memory, and what does it symbolize for you?

The Day You Found Out

Reflect on the moment you learned about your friend's death. Where were you? How did you react? Explore the emotions you felt and how that moment continues to affect you.

A Letter to Your Friend

Write a letter to your friend, expressing everything you wish you could say to them now. This might include memories, apologies, gratitude, or simply sharing how life has changed since they've been gone.

Growing Up Together

Think back to a cherished memory from your childhood with your sibling. How did this moment shape the bond you shared? Now that they are gone, what emotions does this memory stir in you?

The Sibling Bond

Describe the special connection you had with your sibling. How was it different from your relationships with others? Consider how this bond has evolved over time or how you still feel connected to them even after their passing.

The Empty Room

Reflect on the experience of entering your sibling's room after they've passed. What emotions does the space evoke? Which items stand out to you, and what memories do they bring to mind?

A Shared Secret

Think about a secret or inside joke you and your sibling shared. What does this reveal about your relationship? How do you feel now that you're the only one who knows it?

Carrying Their Memory

Explore the ways you keep your sibling's memory alive. Do you carry on any of their traditions or habits? How do you honor their life in your day-to-day routine?

A Significant Day

Recall a significant day you shared with your sibling — whether it was a holiday, birthday, or milestone. How do you remember this day now, and how do you cope with the emotions it brings?

The Last Words You Shared

Think back to the last conversation you had with your sibling. What were the final words exchanged, or were there things left unsaid? How do these words influence your grief?

What I Miss the Most

Reflect on the things you miss most about your sibling. Is it their laugh, their advice, or even the tiny annoyances? How does their absence shape your daily life?

A Letter to My Sibling

Write a letter to your sibling expressing how you feel after their passing. Include the things you wish you could have said, your favorite memories, and the impact of their absence.

Living in Their Shadow

Reflect on how your sibling's death has altered your sense of identity within your family or personally. Do you feel the weight of carrying on their legacy, or do you struggle with the gap they left behind?

The Impact on Family Dynamics

Examine how your sibling's passing has changed your family dynamics. Have your relationships with other family members shifted? What new roles have you taken on, and how do you navigate this new reality?

Their Unfinished Story

Think about the future your sibling had planned or the dreams they were working toward. How do you imagine their life would have unfolded? How do you cope with their story being unfinished?

The Moment of Realization

Write about the moment you realized you were no longer pregnant. Where were you? How did your body and emotions react? Explore the immediate thoughts and feelings that surfaced.

The Decision

Reflect on the process of making the decision to have an

abortion, if applicable. What factors influenced your choice? How did you feel at the time, and how do you think about it now?

What Could Have Been

Imagine what life might have been like if the pregnancy had continued. What do you picture when you think of the child that could have been? How do these thoughts affect your grief or sense of loss?

The Physical Experience

Describe the physical sensations of the miscarriage or abortion. How did your body change, and how did you feel about those changes? How did your body's experience affect your emotional state?

The Unseen Grief

Explore the grief that others may not see or understand. How do you cope with a loss that isn't always acknowledged by society? Write about the ways in which you navigate this unseen grief.

A Letter to the Unborn Child

Write a letter to the child you lost, expressing your feelings, hopes, and regrets. What would you want them to know about your decision, your love, or your pain?

The Impact on Relationships

Reflect on how the miscarriage or abortion has affected your relationships with others, such as a partner, family, or friends. Have these relationships changed? How do you navigate the emotions that arise from these interactions?

The Stigma

Write about the societal or cultural stigma surrounding miscarriage or abortion. How has this stigma impacted your experience or your ability to grieve openly? How do you feel about discussing your experience with others?

The Day That Changed Everything

Focus on the day you learned about the miscarriage or the day of the abortion. What were your thoughts, emotions, and actions? How has this day shaped your life since?

The Lingering Emotions

Explore the lingering emotions that remain after the loss. Do you feel guilt, relief, sorrow, or something else? How do these emotions manifest in your daily life, and how do you cope with them?

The First Moment of Joy

Reflect on the moment you first learned you were going to have a child. What emotions did you feel? How did you imagine the future? Write about the hopes and dreams you had for your child.

The Day Everything Changed

Write about the day you lost your child. What happened, and how did it unfold? Describe your thoughts, emotions, and the immediate impact on your life.

A Letter to Your Child

Write a letter to your child, expressing everything you wish you could say to them. Share your love, memories, and the pain of their absence.

The Empty Space

Describe the physical spaces in your home that remind you

of your child. How has their absence changed these spaces? What memories are tied to these places, and how do you cope with the reminders?

A Memory That Brings You Comfort

Focus on a specific memory of your child that brings you comfort. Describe it in detail, including how it makes you feel now. How do you hold onto this memory?

The Impact on Family Life

Reflect on how the loss of your child has affected your family dynamics. How have your relationships with your partner, other children, or extended family changed? How do you navigate these new dynamics?

A Symbol of Their Life

Choose an object, event, or place that symbolizes your child's life or your memories of them. Describe its significance and how it helps you remember and honor your child.

The Future That Never Was

Imagine the future you had envisioned for your child. Write about the milestones, dreams, and life events you anticipated. How do you reconcile the loss of this future?

Coping with Grief

Explore the ways you cope with the grief of losing your child. What strategies or rituals help you get through the day? How do you manage the waves of grief when they come?

The Things Left Unsaid

Write about the things you wish you had said or done with your child. Are there any regrets or unfinished conversations? How do these thoughts affect your grief?

Honoring Their Memory

Reflect on how you keep your child's memory alive. Do you have rituals, memorials, or traditions that help you feel connected to them? How do these acts of remembrance help you heal?

The Strength to Go On

Write about where you find the strength to continue living after losing your child. What motivates you to keep going? How has this experience changed your perspective on life?

A Glimpse of Them in Everyday Life

Describe moments when you catch a glimpse of your child in everyday life, whether it's in a familiar sound, a similar face, or a shared activity. How do these moments affect you?

Talking to Your Child's Spirit

Imagine having a conversation with your child's spirit or memory. What would you say to them? What would you want them to know about how you've been coping and how much they're missed?

The Journey of Healing

Reflect on your journey of healing since the loss of your child. How have you changed? What has helped you the most in your healing process, and what challenges remain?

The Day You Met

Write about the first time you met your pet. What were your initial impressions? How did your bond begin to form? Reflect on the joy and excitement of bringing them into your life.

A Day in Their Life

Describe a typical day with your pet when they were still with you. What routines did you share? What did they enjoy doing most? How do these memories bring comfort or sadness now?

A Special Memory

Focus on a particular memory that stands out as one of your favorites with your pet. What made this moment unique? How does it encapsulate the bond you shared?

The Last Goodbye

Reflect on the last moments you spent with your pet. What were your thoughts and emotions? How did you say goodbye, and what has stayed with you from that moment?

The Empty Space

Write about the physical space your pet used to occupy in your home. How does the absence of their presence affect you? What reminders of them do you find in your daily life?

The Comfort They Brought

Explore the ways your pet brought comfort, joy, or companionship into your life. How did they help you through tricky times? What role did they play in your emotional well-being?

A Letter to Your Pet

Write a letter to your pet, expressing your love, gratitude, and the pain of losing them. What would you want them to know about how much they meant to you?

The Lessons They Taught You

Reflect on the lessons you learned from your pet. What did they teach you about loyalty, love, or living in the moment?

How have these lessons stayed with you?

The Firsts Without Them

Write about the first time you did something without your pet—whether it was a routine activity, a walk, or coming home to an empty house. How did their absence change the experience?

A Tribute to Their Life

Create a written tribute to your pet, celebrating their life and the joy they brought into yours. What were their quirks, habits, and personality traits that made them unique?

A Place That Reminds You

Describe a place that reminds you of your pet. Maybe it's a park where you took walks together, a favorite spot in the house, or somewhere they loved to visit. How does this place hold their memory?

Imagining Their Voice

If your pet could speak, what do you think they would say to you now? Imagine a conversation with them, where they share their thoughts, feelings, or comfort.

The Impact on Your Daily Life

Reflect on how the loss of your pet has impacted your daily routine. What small moments or activities do you miss the most? How do you adjust to life without them?

The Bond You Shared

Explore the unique bond you had with your pet. How did they understand you in ways that others couldn't? What made your relationship unique, and how do you continue to feel connected to them?

The Healing Process

Write about your journey toward healing after losing your pet. What emotions have you experienced, and how have you navigated them? What helps you remember your pet with love rather than just pain?

Expressing Memories

Write about your favorite memory of the person you've lost. What made that moment special? How do you want to remember them?

Letters to Your Loved One

Write a letter to the person you lost. Share anything you wish you had said or feelings you never expressed. You can tell them about your life now and how you're coping.

Exploring Emotions

Describe the range of emotions you've been feeling since their passing. How have these emotions changed over time? What has surprised you about your reactions?

Finding Strength

Reflect on how you've found the strength to continue each day. What or who has been your anchor during this time? How have you surprised yourself with your resilience?

Writing Through Guilt

If you've experienced feelings of guilt, write about them. What do you feel guilty about? What would you say to someone else in your position?

A Message to Others

Imagine you could offer advice or comfort to someone else who has lost a loved one to suicide. What would you tell them?

How would you help them navigate their grief?

Describing the Person

Write about who your loved one was beyond their struggle. What were their passions, quirks, and joys? How would you like others to remember them?

Imagining a Conversation

Imagine having a conversation with your loved one now. What would you talk about? What would you want them to know?

Future Hopes

Write about how you envision your future as you continue to heal. What steps do you hope to take in your journey of grief and remembrance?

Symbols of Healing

Think about symbols or objects that represent healing or comfort for you. Write about why these symbols are meaningful and how they connect to your loved one.

Movies dealing with Grieving Process

Manchester by the Sea (2016) – This film follows a man who returns to his hometown after the death of his brother and must confront his past along with the grief that has haunted him.

A Ghost Story (2017) – A unique take on grief, this film follows a recently deceased ghost who watches over his grieving widow and observes the passage of time.

The Lovely Bones (2009) – Based on Alice Sebold's novel, this story is about a young girl who watches over her family and her murder investigation from the afterlife.

Rabbit Hole (2010) – This film deals with the aftermath of a child's death and shows how the parents struggle to find a way forward in the wake of their loss.

The Tree of Life (2011) – While not solely focused on grief, this philosophical film by Terrence Malick explores themes of life, loss, and existence.

Hereditary (2018) – A psychological horror that delves into family grief as they grapple with both tragic and supernatural events.

Brokeback Mountain (2005) – A story of deep and complex love, this film also addresses the personal grief and challenges faced by its characters over time.

The Farewell (2019) – This film follows a Chinese-American woman who returns to China under the guise of a fake wedding to say goodbye to her terminally ill grandmother secretly.

Steel Magnolias (1989) – A blend of humor and heartbreak, this movie showcases a close-knit group of Southern women as they cope with the loss of a beloved friend and family member.

Eternal Sunshine of the Spotless Mind (2004) – While primarily a film about relationships and memory, it also explores the emotional grief and pain of losing someone you love.

Poems that deal with Grief

Do Not Go Gentle into That Good Night by Dylan Thomas – A passionate plea to fight against death and the inevitable. This poem captures the intensity of facing loss and the desire to hold onto life.

Funeral Blues by W.H. Auden – Known for its iconic opening line, *Stop all the clocks*, this poem poignantly expresses the profound sense of loss and the all-encompassing impact of death on the world.

In Memoriam A.H.H. by Alfred Lord Tennyson – Written in memory of Tennyson's close friend Arthur Hallam, this long poem grapples with deep sorrow and the poet's search for solace, reflecting on personal grief.

The Layers by Stanley Kunitz – This poem reflects on the process of living through and coming to terms with grief, emphasizing resilience and how time shapes our experience of loss.

One Art by Elizabeth Bishop – A meditation on the art of losing, this poem intertwines resignation and pain, exploring how loss, both minor and major, permeates life.

When Death Comes by Mary Oliver – Oliver's reflective piece intertwines life and death, offering a contemplative perspective on mortality and the inevitability of grief while finding meaning in life's fleeting nature.

Elegy by John Donne – This reflective poem delves into the nature of death and grief, posing existential questions about loss and mortality with deep spiritual overtones.

Annabel Lee by Edgar Allan Poe – This haunting poem explores the depth of love and the sorrow of losing a beloved, capturing an enduring sense of grief and loss.

Grief by Susan Mitchell – A contemporary and raw exploration of grief, this poem addresses the emotional weight of loss and the complexities that come with mourning a loved one.

The Peace of Wild Things by Wendell Berry – Though not

exclusively about grief, this poem offers a soothing reflection on finding peace amidst struggles and the pain that life inevitably brings.

The Lovely Bones by Alice Sebold – This novel follows a young girl who, after being murdered, watches over her family from the afterlife, exploring themes of grief and healing from both the perspective of the deceased and her family.

A Man Called Ove by Fredrik Backman – While primarily about a grumpy older man, the story delves into Ove's grief over his wife's death and the emotional journey he embarks on as he reconnects with life and neighbors.

The Year of Magical Thinking by Joan Didion – This memoir (not a novel) provides a powerful and personal exploration of grief after the sudden death of Didion's husband, as well as the serious illness of their daughter.

The Light We Lost by Jill Santopolo – This novel examines the enduring impact of loss, exploring how grief shapes the choices and relationships of the characters over time.

Bridge of Clay by Markus Zusak – A family grapples with the death of their mother in this novel, dealing with the emotional complexities of grief as they try to move forward together.

The Ocean at the End of the Lane by Neil Gaiman – Blending fantasy and reality, this novel explores childhood grief and how its emotional weight lingers into adulthood.

The Immortalists by Chloe Benjamin – Following four siblings who learn the dates of their deaths, this novel examines how knowledge of mortality influences their lives and their experiences with grief.

All the Light We Cannot See by Anthony Doerr – Set during World War II, this novel highlights characters who experience profound loss and grief as they navigate the devastation and chaos of war.

A Grief Observed by C.S. Lewis – Though a memoir, this work offers a raw and honest reflection on Lewis's personal grief after his wife's death, providing deep insight into the mourning process.

The Hours by Michael Cunningham – This novel weaves together the stories of three women whose lives are connected through Virginia Woolf's *Mrs. Dalloway*, exploring themes of loss, depression, and the search for meaning

Songs that deal with Grief

Tears in Heaven by Eric Clapton

This heartfelt song was written by Clapton after the tragic loss of his son. It reflects on grief and the longing to be reunited with a loved one.

Hurt by Johnny Cash (Cover of Nine Inch Nails)

Cash's cover of this song adds a deep, haunting quality to the themes of pain, regret, and loss, making it a poignant reflection on grief.

See You Again by Wiz Khalifa ft. Charlie Puth

Written as a tribute to the late actor Paul Walker, this song touches on the sadness of losing someone and the hope of meeting them again.

My Heart Will Go On by Celine Dion

This iconic song from the movie *Titanic* captures the deep emotions of loss and remembrance.

One Sweet Day by Mariah Carey & Boyz II Men

A collaboration that speaks to the pain of losing someone close and the hope of reuniting with them in the afterlife.

I Will Remember You by Sarah McLachlan

It is a melancholic song about remembering a loved one who is no longer around, capturing both the pain and beauty of memories.

Wake Me Up When September Ends by Green Day

Written by Billie Joe Armstrong about the loss of his father, this song explores themes of grief, longing, and the passage of time.

Someone Like You by Adele

Although this song is about the end of a relationship, its themes of loss, sorrow, and moving on resonate with those grieving the absence of a loved one.

Candle in the Wind by Elton John

Initially written in memory of Marilyn Monroe and later re-recorded as a tribute to Princess Diana, this song speaks to the sadness of losing someone who touched the lives of many.

The Night We Met by Lord Huron

This haunting song captures the longing and grief of missing someone who was once a significant part of your life.

Affirmation Books for Grief

Healing After Loss: Daily Meditations for Working Through Grief by Martha Whitmore Hickman

This book offers daily meditations that provide comfort and hope for those grieving the loss of a loved one. Each meditation includes an affirmation or thought for the day, helping readers find a sense of peace and healing.

Grief One Day at a Time: 365 Meditations to Help You Heal After Loss by Alan D. Wolfelt

This book provides daily affirmations and meditations designed to support those who are grieving. Each day presents a short, reflective passage, followed by an affirmation to guide readers through their grief journey.

Comfort for the Grieving Spouse's Heart: Hope and Healing After Losing Your Partner by Gary Roe

Focused on those grieving the loss of a spouse, this book includes affirmations and reflections that offer comfort, hope, and encouragement. It's designed to help readers navigate the pain of loss while finding strength and healing.

Hope in the Mourning: Encouraging Affirmations for the Grieving Heart by Marla Alupoaicei

This book offers a collection of affirmations and prayers tailored explicitly to those grieving the loss of a loved one. Each affirmation is intended to bring comfort and hope during difficult times.

The Grief Recovery Handbook by John W. James and Russell Friedman

While not solely focused on affirmations, this book provides practical advice and emotional support for those dealing with grief. It includes exercises and reflections to help readers process their loss and begin the healing journey.

I Wasn't Ready to Say Goodbye: Surviving, Coping, and Healing After the Sudden Death of a Loved One by Brook Noel and Pamela D. Blair

You Can Heal Your Heart: Finding Peace After a Breakup, Divorce, or Death by Louise Hay and David Kessler

Co-authored by renowned affirmation expert Louise Hay, this book blends affirmations with practical advice for healing after a significant loss. It helps readers navigate complex emotions with compassion and hope.

A Year of Positive Thinking for Grief and Loss: Daily Affirmations to Bring Comfort and Strength by Cyndie Spiegel

This book offers a year's worth of daily affirmations specifically for those experiencing grief and loss. It is designed to bring comfort, strength, and positivity to those navigating their grief journey.

Types of Therapy that help with Grief

Grief Counseling

This form of therapy explicitly addresses the emotions and challenges related to grief. It helps individuals express their feelings, process their loss, and find ways to adjust to life without their loved ones.

Techniques: Talking about the deceased, exploring memories, identifying and expressing emotions, and developing coping strategies.

Cognitive Behavioral Therapy (CBT)

CBT helps individuals identify and change negative thought patterns that may contribute to feelings of grief and depression. It's useful for those who might be struggling with guilt, anger, or regret after a loss.

Techniques: Challenging irrational thoughts, practicing mindfulness, and engaging in activities that improve mood and well-being.

Complicated Grief Therapy (CGT)

CGT is designed for those who experience prolonged or intense grief that disrupts their daily functioning, known as complicated grief. It combines elements of CBT with techniques that address the specific challenges of complicated grief.

Techniques: Revisiting memories of the deceased, re-engaging with life, and creating rituals to honor the loss.

Narrative Therapy

Narrative therapy helps individuals reshape their story of loss by exploring and reframing the narrative they have constructed around their grief. It emphasizes the individual's own strengths and resilience.

Techniques*:* Writing or talking about the loss in a way that highlights personal growth, resilience, and the positive aspects of the relationship with the deceased.

Art Therapy

Art therapy uses creative expression to help individuals process their emotions and grief. It's beneficial for those who may have difficulty verbalizing their feelings.

Techniques: Drawing, painting, sculpting, or other forms of artistic expression to explore and express grief-related emotions.

Mindfulness-Based Stress Reduction (MBSR)

MBSR combines mindfulness meditation and yoga to help individuals manage the physical and emotional symptoms of grief. It encourages living in the present moment and accepting emotions without judgment.

Techniques: Mindfulness meditation, body scanning, yoga, and breathing exercises to reduce stress and increase emotional awareness.

Support Groups

Support groups offer a communal approach to grieving, where individuals can share their experiences with others who have experienced similar losses. This provides emotional support, validation, and a sense of community.

Techniques: Group discussions, sharing stories, mutual support, and sometimes structured activities led by a facilitator.

Existential Therapy

Existential therapy addresses the big questions that often arise after a loss, such as the meaning of life, death, and personal existence. It helps individuals find meaning and purpose in their lives after experiencing a significant loss.

Techniques: Deep reflection on life's meaning, exploring values, and discussing the concepts of mortality and purpose.

Acceptance and Commitment Therapy (ACT)

ACT encourages individuals to accept their grief and the emotions that come with it rather than trying to avoid or suppress them. It also helps individuals commit to actions that align with their values, even in the face of grief.

Techniques: Mindfulness exercises, cognitive defusion, values clarification, and committed action.

Eye Movement Desensitization and Reprocessing (EMDR)

Originally developed for trauma, EMDR can be effective for processing the intense emotional pain of grief. It helps individuals reprocess distressing memories associated with the loss in a way that reduces their emotional charge. *Techniques:* Bilateral stimulation (such as eye movements or tapping) while recalling traumatic or distressing memories to mitigate their impact.

Psychoanalytic or Psychodynamic Therapy

These therapies explore how unresolved conflicts, often from childhood, may influence an individual's current experience of grief. They help individuals understand the deeper emotional underpinnings of their grief.

Techniques: Free association, dream analysis, and exploring relationships and past experiences to gain insight into current feelings of despair.

Holidays can be particularly challenging for those grieving the loss of a loved one, as they often bring back memories and highlight the absence of the person who has passed away. Creating rituals can help honor their memory while providing comfort and a sense of connection during this difficult time. Here are some rituals that can help with grief during the holidays:

Create a Memory Ornament

Make or buy an ornament that symbolizes your loved one. This could include their photo, a small note, or something that reminds you of them. Hanging this ornament on your holiday tree can serve as a way to include them in your celebrations.

Light a Candle in Their Honor

Light a candle at your holiday table or in a special place in your home in memory of your loved one. You can do this each night of the holiday season or on a specific day that holds significance.

Set a Place at the Table

Set an empty place at the dinner table to honor your loved one's memory. This can be a powerful visual reminder that they are still with you in spirit.

Share a Favorite Story or Memory

During a holiday gathering, invite family and friends to share a favorite story or memory of the person who has passed away. This can be a meaningful way to keep their spirit alive and connect with others who are also grieving.

Create a Memory Box or Scrapbook

Put together a box or scrapbook filled with photos, letters, and mementos that remind you of your loved one. You can revisit it during the holidays, adding new memories or reflections each year.

Donate or Volunteer in Their Name

Consider donating to a charity that is meaningful to your loved one or volunteering your time to a cause they care about. This act of giving can help channel your grief into something positive and honor your legacy.

Write a Letter to Your Loved One

Write a letter to your loved one expressing how much you miss them, what the holidays are like without them, and any other thoughts or feelings you wish to share. You can place the letter in a special spot, burn it as a symbolic release, or keep it in a journal.

Cook Their Favorite Holiday Dish

Prepare a dish that your loved one enjoyed or that they used to make during the holidays. Sharing it with others can bring a sense of closeness and keep their traditions alive.

Visit a Special Place

If possible, visit a place that is meaningful to your loved one, such as their gravesite, a favorite park, or another special location. Spend some quiet time there reflecting, praying, or simply being present.

Create a Memory Tree

Set up a small tree dedicated to your loved one. Decorate it with ornaments, notes, and photos that remind you of them. This can be a focal point in your home where you can reflect on your memories.

Play Their Favorite Music

Incorporate your loved one's favorite holiday music into your celebrations. This can be comforting and a way to feel their presence during the holidays.

Perform an Act of Kindness

In memory of your loved one, perform a random act of kindness during the holiday season. This could be anything from paying for someone's coffee to helping a neighbor. Acts of kindness can bring a sense of purpose and connection.

Host a Remembrance Gathering

Invite close family and friends to a small gathering dedicated to remembering your loved one. You can light candles, share stories, and support each other in your grief.

Create a Holiday Altar

Set up a small altar or table with photos, candles, and items that remind you of your loved one. This can be a space where you go to reflect, meditate, or simply feel connected to them during the holiday season.

Start a New Tradition

Create a new tradition in honor of your loved one. This could be something as simple as taking a walk-in nature, baking cookies in their favorite shape, or having a quiet moment of reflection each holiday season.

Write a Gratitude List

While acknowledging the pain of loss, write a list of things you are grateful for that were connected to your loved one. Reflect on the positive impact they had on your life and how those memories can bring you comfort.

Release a Lantern or Balloon

On a special holiday night, release a lantern or biodegradable balloon into the sky in memory of your loved one. This can be a symbolic gesture of letting go while also sending your thoughts and love to them.

Create a Photo Display

Set up a display of photos of your loved one in your home. This can be a temporary setup just for the holidays or a permanent part of your decor, where you can honor their memory each day.

Watch Their Favorite Holiday Movie

Watch a holiday movie that your loved one enjoyed. This can be a way to feel connected to them and to bring a sense of joy and remembrance to your holiday celebrations.

Practice Self-Care

Remember to take care of yourself during the holiday season. Grief can be exhausting, so make time for activities that bring you peace and comfort, whether it's a warm bath, a walk in nature, or simply resting.

These rituals can help you honor the memory of your loved one while also finding ways to cope with the unique challenges that the holiday season can bring when you are grieving.

Self-Care Techniques

Mourning is an incredibly challenging time, and self-care can play a crucial role in managing the emotional and physical toll of grief. Here are some self-care techniques that can be helpful during mourning:

Emotional Self-Care

Allow Yourself to Grieve

Permit yourself to feel and express your emotions. It's okay to cry, be angry, or feel overwhelmed. Recognize that grief is a process with its own timeline.

Journal Your Feelings

Writing about your thoughts and emotions can help you process grief and identify patterns in your feelings. Journaling also offers a private space for reflection.

Seek Support

Connect with friends, family, or a support group. Sharing your feelings with those who understand can provide comfort and validation.

Practice Mindfulness and Meditation

Engage in mindfulness or meditation practices to ground yourself and manage overwhelming emotions. Apps like *Headspace* or *Calm* offer helpful guided sessions.

Set Small Goals

Establish small, manageable goals each day. This can be as

simple as getting out of bed, taking a shower, or going for a short walk.

Physical Self-Care

Ensure you get adequate rest and sleep. Grief can be exhausting, and maintaining a regular sleep schedule helps manage fatigue and emotional stress.

Eat Nourishing Foods

Focus on eating balanced, nutritious meals. Even though grief can affect your appetite, try to maintain a healthy diet to support your overall well-being.

Stay Hydrated

Drink plenty of water to keep your body hydrated. Dehydration can affect your mood and energy levels.

Engage in Gentle Exercise

Incorporate gentle physical activity like walking, stretching, or yoga into your routine. Exercise can help improve mood and reduce stress.

Mental and Spiritual Self-Care

Practice Relaxation Techniques

Use relaxation techniques such as deep breathing exercises or progressive muscle relaxation to calm your mind and body.

Create a Comforting Ritual

Develop a personal ritual to honor your loved one— lighting a candle, visiting a particular place, or engaging in an activity they enjoyed.

Engage in Creative Outlets

Express your emotions through creative activities like

drawing, painting, or playing music. Creative expression can be therapeutic for processing grief.

Read or Listen to Inspirational Material

Engage with books, podcasts, or other resources that offer comfort and perspective on grief and healing.

Practical Self-Care

Establish a Routine

Create a daily routine to provide structure and a sense of normalcy. This can help you manage day-to-day life while mourning.

Limit Stressful Activities

Reduce or avoid activities that add stress or anxiety during this time. Focus on what you can handle, and give yourself permission to step back from overwhelming responsibilities.

Seek Professional Help

If your grief feels overwhelming or disrupts your ability to function, consider reaching out to a mental health professional who specializes in grief counseling.

Set Boundaries

Set boundaries regarding what you're comfortable with during this time. It's okay to say no to invitations or requests that feel too overwhelming.

Engage in Activities You Enjoy

Spend time doing activities that bring you joy or relaxation—whether it's reading, gardening, or watching a favorite show. These can provide a temporary break from grief.

Practice Self-Compassion

Be kind to yourself and recognize that mourning is a complicated process. Avoid self-criticism, and acknowledge that it's okay to have both good and bad days.

Create a Gratitude Practice

Focus on minor aspects of life for which you are grateful, even in difficult times. This can help shift your focus and foster a sense of hope.

www.ingramcontent.com/pod-product-compliance
Lightning Source LLC
Chambersburg PA
CBHW020357130626
46549CB00006B/2323